THE LAST
THREE MILES

THE LAST
THREE MILES

POLITICS, MURDER, AND THE

CONSTRUCTION OF AMERICA'S

FIRST SUPERHIGHWAY

Steven Hart

THE NEW PRESS

NEW YORK
LONDON

*Overleaf: aerial shot of the Pulaski Skyway is courtesy of
the Newark Public Library*

Requests for permission to reproduce selections
from this book should be mailed to:
Permissions Department, The New Press, 38 Greene Street, New York, NY 10013.

Published in the United States by The New Press, New York, 2007
Distributed by W. W. Norton & Company, Inc., New York

LIBRARY OF CONGRESS CATALOGING-IN-PUBLICATION DATA

Hart, Steven, 1958–
   The last three miles : politics, murder, and the construction of America's first
superhighway / Steven Hart.
      p.   cm.
   Includes bibliographical references and index.
   ISBN 978-1-59558-098-6 (hc.)
   1. Pulaski Skyway (N.J.)—Design and construction—History.   I. Title.

TG425.H37 2007
388. 10979'26—dc22   2006033820

The New Press was established in 1990 as a not-for-profit alternative to the large, commercial
publishing houses currently dominating the book publishing industry. The New Press operates in the public interest rather than for private gain, and is committed to publishing, in innovative ways, works of educational, cultural, and community value that are often deemed
insufficiently profitable.

www.thenewpress.com

Composition by dix!
This book was set in Walbaum MT

Printed in the United States of America

2   4   6   8   10   9   7   5   3   1

CONTENTS

For Mary, who fights the good fight,
and for Carolyn and Torgyn,
who make the fight worthwhile.

Introduction

The construction of Route 25 [Pulaski Skyway] in New Jersey is an introduction into the transportation system of a new kind of link that is something between "highway" and "railway." This new member of the transportation family may be called "superhighway."

—D. P. Krynine, engineer, *Transactions of the American Society of Civil Engineers, 1931*

This three-mile highway, reaching 135 feet into the air, is also a rare combination of artistic planning with structural solidity. . . . It is a thing of use, a thing of convenience. It brings cities near, bridges not two but all the states more closely.

—*Newark Evening News,* editorial, November 23, 1932

That was a terrible time, when they were building the Skyway. Those guys who were picketing, they were fighting for their jobs. And they all got thrown in jail. My grandfather probably would've been thrown in jail, too, except he got shot in the back and they had to take him to the hospital instead.

—Jim Bergin, ironworker

America at the dawn of the 1930s was a land of astonishingly grim contrasts. The Depression was sinking its claws deep into society, breadlines were stretching across cities, and factories that had been humming along only a year or two earlier were barely operating, or sitting idle. In a few years, whole regions of the United States would be depopulated as their inhabitants took to the road in search of work. An entire "Bonus Army" of destitute veterans of the Great War would gather in the nation's capital to ask for early payment of money promised to them by Congress, only to be chased out by bayonet-wielding soldiers as the smoke from their burning shantytowns floated past the Capitol dome.

And yet, the heroic era of public works—which had begun with the completion of the Eads Bridge across the Mississippi River in 1874 and the Brooklyn Bridge in 1883—was about to see its high noon. At the same time, new construction techniques were allowing office buildings to become grander and taller. It might have seemed that America's future was in doubt, but the trappings of that future were rising all over the country.

In Manhattan, excavation work on the foundation for the Empire State Building began in January 1930. On the other side of the continent, preliminary work on the Golden Gate Bridge spanning the entrance to San Francisco Bay began in November 1930, followed by the San Francisco–Oakland Bay Bridge. A few months later, in a sun-blasted canyon on the Nevada-Arizona border, laborers started tunneling a new channel for the Colorado River, thus clearing the way for construction of the immense white wall of the Hoover Dam. That same year, the first in a system of "spillways" designed to buffer the force of floodwaters from the Mississippi River was completed at Bonnet Carre, about thirty miles north of New Orleans; a few years later it protected the Crescent City from what would have been a disastrous flood. The transformation of America from a country of railways and local roads to a nation of automobile highways and steel bridges was well under way. And amid all this feverish energy, one of the great accomplishments of the age—the complete linkage of Manhattan, the economic center of the United States, with automobile traffic from the mainland—was about to be realized.

Though a limited underground rail system between Jersey City, New Jersey, and New York City—the "Hudson Tubes"— had been running since 1908, America was now a realm of cars and trucks with no direct access to Manhattan on the far shore of the Hudson River. The first step to defeating that river barrier had come in 1927 with the opening of the Holland Tunnel, which allowed automobile traffic to pass between lower Manhattan and Jersey City. A few dozen miles to the north, the George Washington Bridge would begin taking traffic in 1931. And when the first tube of the Lincoln Tunnel opened in 1937, Manhattan became the center of a vast highway infrastructure that would remain essentially unchanged well into the next century, governing the daily lives of hundreds of thousands of drivers and shaping the way the residents of three states worked, played, and raised their children.

As the pieces of this immense transportation puzzle were welded, hammered, and blasted into place, an even wider network of concrete and asphalt was taking shape that would carry the nation's drivers to this vital series of crossings. The crucial link in this network was a thirteen-mile extension of Route 1 from Elizabeth, New Jersey, that would funnel traffic from points south and west of Manhattan right to the mouth of the Holland Tunnel, and help disperse the flood tide of westbound cars and trucks that daily erupted from the tunnel and eddied on the narrow, crowded streets of Jersey City.

Most of the work on this highway extension had already

been completed by the time the Depression took hold. The final and most crucial portion was a roughly three-mile stretch of elevated highway that would connect the outskirts of Newark with the edge of Jersey City. This would become the visual keystone of a new kind of road that required a new word to describe it: superhighway. Building it would take two years, fifteen lives, $21 million, a labor war, and a murder trial that marked the turning point in the long reign of America's most powerful and ruthless political bosses.

During its design and construction in the 1920s and early 1930s, this crucial stretch of America's first superhighway was known by several names: Meadowlands Viaduct, Diagonal Highway, High-Level Viaduct. Not until 1933, a year after it opened for public use, did it become known as the General Casimir Pulaski Memorial Skyway, or simply the Pulaski Skyway.

Though it is not as celebrated or loved as, say, the Brooklyn Bridge or the George Washington Bridge, the Skyway deserves an equal if not greater place in the public memory, for it played an even more crucial role in the development of the nation's traffic infrastructure—it helps cars reach those more famous bridges.

The Skyway's hybrid design, combining a long elevated highway across the southernmost point of the immense swamp called the New Jersey Meadowlands with two bridges spanning the Hackensack and Passaic rivers, just north of their confluence at the top of Newark Bay, marked it as a different kind of road, one of several taking shape across the country that reflected the growth of the automobile from a rich man's hobby to a middle-class mainstay. From this point forward, major highways would no longer simply serve communities— they would also dominate them, shape them, and, sometimes, degrade them or kill them off entirely.

When it opened in 1932, in a Thanksgiving Day gala, the Skyway was hailed as a marvel of engineering. Newspaper editorials praised it in terms that would have been considered lavish for a cathedral or national monument; traffic planners offered calculations in which days, weeks, and months of time could now be regained by drivers who had once been mired in traffic-glutted local roads; engineers surveyed the Skyway's curious blend of elegance and black-steel brutality and pronounced it a thing of beauty. Much of what was said back then remains true today—the Pulaski Skyway is a milestone in the early history of America's effort to cope with the rise of the automobile.

It is also a monument to failure.

New technology is frequently viewed in terms of the old technology it most closely resembles. Just as the first automobiles traveled along roads better suited to horse-and-buggy traffic, the first improvements designed to handle the flow of automobiles were influenced by railroads—the only other form of high-speed cross-country traffic known at the time. The flaws incorporated into the design of the Pulaski Skyway were completely understandable, even predictable, in terms of the existing technology. They also rendered the structure almost instantly useless for much of its sole purpose. Trucks had to be barred from its narrow lanes; the cars and buses that were still allowed to use the span came to grief so often that the editorialists who had praised the Skyway as a highway to the stars began calling it "Death Avenue."

Ironically, the Pulaski Skyway had already earned that title for another kind of calamity—a brutal labor war that bloodied the grounds over which the Skyway passed, and proved to be a turning point in the career of one of America's most powerful and least understood political figures: Frank Hague, mayor of Jersey City, boss of the Hudson County Democratic organization, and power broker with enough clout to choose governors, sway legislatures, and intimidate presidents.

Hague had (and has) his defenders, but even the staunchest of them admit that the Skyway conflict set the stage for the ugliest incident of his career. This labor war, referred to by local newspapers as "the War of the Meadows," pitted desperate union men against one of the most violently antiunion industrial groups in American history. The battles were fought with the kind of weapons used by men with few resources: clubs, knives, metal pipes, and—appropriately for the project— fistfuls of heavy steel rivets. And when a man was killed in one of the skirmishes, Hague responded with an abuse of power so massive that it ruined scores of lives, financially destroyed one of his most ardent supporters, transformed Jersey City from a union haven to a domain of sweatshops, and turned Hague himself into something resembling the monster his enemies had always claimed him to be.

The story of the Skyway is the story of an entire country suddenly scrambling to keep pace with the changes wrought by a technological innovation—in this case, affordable, mass-produced automobiles. The great steeplechase race known as progress, already grueling enough, was about to shift into overdrive: other transforming innovations and more struggles were not far off. In order to reinvent itself as a nation of paved roads and small cars, America produced an impressive network of roads and bridges within a relatively brief span of time. The construction of an even more astonishing web of interstate highways was still a generation away, but the stage for it was set here.

The story of the Skyway is also emblematic of a nation coming to grips with the fact that the homespun safety nets of an agrarian society simply could not withstand the strains of mass immigration, the explosive growth of cities, and the desperate poverty of the Depression. This realization would lead to the creation of Social Security and an array of other government programs, and ensured that the America emerging from the Depression was a strikingly different country from the one that entered it. The Skyway, in symbolic terms and perhaps in others as well, is a bridge between those two eras.

It is also a deeply saddening chapter in the fitful struggle between capital and labor, and between employer and employee— a struggle that lasted longer than the cold war and affected America every bit as deeply. Though it involved demands that now seem only reasonable—bearable working hours, a measure of job security, some protection against an employer's whims—it was fought with an intensity that approached civil warfare in a Third World country. And it has largely been banished from public consciousness. The battle songs that reminded workers of the recent, bloody past—"Joe Hill," "Which Side Are You On?"—are now laughed off as fodder for overly earnest folksingers; the work of brave men and women facing the combined power of government and business has been submerged in stereotypes of crooked labor bosses like Jimmy Hoffa and Jackie Presser. During the Skyway labor war, a man denounced as a dictator and a gangster frequently acted with integrity and good conscience, while another man elevated to civic leadership and national influence used his power like a back-alley thug.

Some incidents can be used as a lens to examine the place and the time in which they occurred. The story of the Skyway labor war offers such a lens. It is a story that encompasses laborers, engineers, gangsters, and presidents. The story reaches all the way up to the White House, but it begins deep underground.

CHAPTER 1

The Three Barriers

We should have a right to ask that this people which has tamed
a continent, which has built up a country with a continent for
its base, which boasts itself with truth as the mightiest Republic the world has ever seen . . . we should have a right to demand that such a nation build good roads.

—President Theodore Roosevelt (1903)

Early in the afternoon of October 29, 1924, the shock wave
from a dynamite explosion rippled through the silt and rock at
the bottom of the Hudson River. Two crews, tunneling from
the opposite banks—Canal Street in Manhattan and the Erie
Railroad yards in Jersey City—had come within a few feet of
each other after two years of labor beneath the river. The final
blast cleared away the remaining rock and muck, and suddenly
it was possible to walk from New York to New Jersey.

The foremen of the two crews also happened to be brothers:
Harry Redwood of the New York crew, and Norman Redwood
of the New Jersey work gang. They reached through the five-
foot hole to clasp hands, grinning broadly, a hundred feet
below the surface of the river.

Two years later, another handshake took place at the midway point beneath the river. The men clasping hands were the governors of the states linked by the tunnel, and on either side of them stood the commissioners appointed by New York and New Jersey to oversee the tunnel project. The photo session was the climax of an August 21, 1926, inspection tour in which the dignitaries walked along a passage now lined with tiles, paved, fully lighted, and ventilated by an innovative system of air shafts and blowers that would keep the tunnel clear of exhaust fumes from the steady flow of cars and trucks.

The men—all looking dapper in suits and high collars, most clutching fashionable Panama hats—arrayed themselves on either side of the mosaic tile boundary where New York theoretically meets New Jersey. Alfred E. Smith, serving his second term as the governor of New York, reached across the line to clasp hands with A. Harry Moore, likewise serving his second term as governor of New Jersey.

The two Democrats were also brothers of a sort in that they were products of political machines. Al Smith was a son of Tammany Hall, the New York Democratic club that took its name from a Delaware Indian chief and styled its officers as sachems and braves. A. Harry Moore was from Tammany's mirror image across the river: the Hudson County machine controlled by Jersey City mayor Frank Hague. A close friend of Smith, Hague would work for many years to acquire some of the easygoing style that came so naturally to the "Happy Warrior" of Tammany Hall.

The Holland Tunnel opened to cars and trucks at midnight on November 12–13, 1927. The weekend of the opening set off orgies of civic boosterism on either side of the tunnel. On the evening of Saturday, November 12, the tunnel was opened to pedestrians for two hours, during which time a pageant of civic leaders, area residents, and even a couple of marching bands ranged back and forth along the echoing passage. At 7 p.m. the tunnel was closed to foot traffic, and the Jersey City spectators headed to a fireworks show up the hill from the tunnel entrance.

The first fifty-cent toll was paid at midnight by Brigadier General George R. Dyer, chairman of the New York State Bridge and Tunnel Commission. A total of 51,748 vehicles passed through the tunnel on its first day. The Hudson River crossing, a passage that could take a half hour or longer by ferry, could now be accomplished in minutes.

But automobiles, having crossed one barrier, met a second as soon as they arrived in Jersey City and tried to head west: a tangle of narrow, traffic-clogged local roads, and a vast swamp beyond it. Cars and trucks bound for points west headed up the slope of Bergen Hill to Hudson Boulevard, the long avenue that ran along the spine of Hudson County. From there, they joined the lines of cars and horse-drawn carts working their way along Communipaw Avenue and the frequently opened drawbridges spanning the Hackensack and Passaic rivers. Even after 1930, when the inauguration of the H. Otto Wittpenn Bridge across the Hackensack River afforded some measure of relief, it could take westbound drivers as long as three hours to reach Newark—a distance of only four miles. In what would become the enduring theme of the automobile age, increased capacity in one area had created a bottleneck in another.

The bulk of Hudson County presents itself on maps as an irregular spear of land pointing at a slight southwest angle. It is bounded on the east by the Hudson River as it flows into Upper New York Bay; on the south by the narrow waterway called Kill Van Kull and Staten Island; and on the west by Newark Bay and the southern extreme of the Meadowlands, the huge swamp that has given New Yorkers (and hence the rest of the world) the image of New Jersey as a toxic marshland.

Jersey City dominates the center of the key-shaped peninsula; Bayonne occupies the extreme southern tip. North of Jersey City, the county becomes a patchwork of smaller cities: Hoboken, Union City, Weehawken, North Bergen, and West New York. The western portion of Hudson County extends into the Meadowlands proper to encompass Secaucus and Kearny.

A crow flapping due west from Battery Park in lower Manhattan would fly first over the Hudson River and the upper reaches of New York Bay, then the shoreline of Jersey City and the low trap rock ridge dubbed Bergen Hill by the early Dutch settlers—*bergen* being the Dutch word for a safe place—and now known to Jersey City residents as the Heights. That hill continues to the north, rising to join the spectacular Palisades.

Crossing Bergen Hill, the crow would pass over the Hackensack River, which meanders at a southwestern angle toward Newark Bay, and then the Passaic River, similarly meandering along a southeastern course to the same destination. The crow would then reach the northern end of Newark and the suburbs of Kearny and North Arlington, where an eight-mile-long ridge defines the western rim of the Meadowlands.

The thirty-two-square-mile basin of the Meadowlands, which tapers to a point at the head of Newark Bay, was viewed alternately as a garbage dump by New York City and the developing communities of northern New Jersey, and as a hindrance to travel. Its ponds bred clouds of mosquitoes so voracious that during the Colonial era, local farmers would punish disobedient slaves by leaving them chained in the open overnight. Travelers from New York in the 1700s often paused a few days in Newark so their horses could "blood up" after enduring the insect assault on the dirt roads crossing the area.

It was time-consuming but not impossible to cross the Meadowlands. Coaches crisscrossed the Meadowlands between "stages," stopping-off points where passengers would board a new coach with a fresh team of horses. One of the oldest roads in the country crosses the swamp, linking Paterson and Hoboken, and still bears the name of its original surface material: Paterson Plank Road. But the pace of travel across the marshes picked up only in the nineteenth century, when railroad tracks and trolley lines were cut through the creeks and quagmires. The western bank of the Hudson River—what would come to be known as the "gold coast"—bristled with ferry slips and railroad terminals. By the end of the nineteenth century, the waters of the Hudson River and Upper New York Bay were a riot of lighters, cargo ships, and tugboats, roiled by the occasional ocean liner or military vessel. The density of cross-river traffic was about to reach critical mass concurrent with the arrival of a noisy, sputtering technological interloper that seemed to inspire equal measures of love and hatred—another recurring theme of the automobile age.

It seems strange now, but the unbreakable union of Americans and automobiles was not a case of love at first sight.

The first cars were unlovely things: loud, smelly, demanding to operate, and difficult to keep going once they were started. Drivers went out muffled in hats, goggles, and travel clothes; as often as not they returned mummified in mud and road dust. The engine noise frightened horses and aggravated anyone else using the road. Cars were regularly denounced as dangerous toys for people with too much money. The sight of a goggled motorist clattering down the street was "a picture of the arrogance of wealth," groused Woodrow Wilson in 1908, while he was president of Princeton University. "Nothing has spread socialistic feeling more in this country than the automobile."

Henry Ford, with his aggressive pricing strategies and standardized designs, is rightly credited with putting cars within the reach of the middle class. Ford's company was not the first automobile firm in the United States: that position is held by the Duryea Motor Wagon Company of Peoria, Illinois, launched in 1895 by Charles Duryea. But Ford's endless tinkering produced the first popular mass-market car: the Model T, first marketed late in 1908. Yet the Model T still required a degree of athleticism to operate: the driver had to hand-crank the engine from the front, then leap behind the steering wheel to manipulate the choke. During cranking, the engine could backfire with enough force to break the operator's wrist; if the car stalled, the whole routine had to be repeated. This was only the beginning of the Model T's eccentricities, which seem to have inspired as much affection as exasperation, and called forth great wellsprings of ingenuity from its owners. Celebrations of the Model T and its quirks are a lively subgenre of American literature, highlighted by E. B. White's 1936 essay "Farewell to Model T" and an amusing chapter of John Steinbeck's 1945 novel *Cannery Row*, in which a driver solves a technical challenge by completing a ride through the countryside in reverse gear.

It remained for Charles F. Kettering to design the first reliable self-starter, which appeared in the Cadillac in 1912. Demountable rim- and cord-tires followed, making it easier to change flat tires and making a car trip that much less of an adventure.

But the car truly began to transform America when enclosed vehicles became affordable. Enclosed cars, which provided shelter from the elements and privacy for young couples, accounted for only 2 percent of the vehicles sold in 1916; ten years later, they accounted for three-quarters of all sales.

The love affair had begun. And, as with most love affairs, one of the involved parties soon felt the need for a makeover. That makeover would take the form of ribbons of asphalt crisscrossing the countryside.

Cars were fixtures of the twentieth century, but America's roads remained fixed in the nineteenth. Most of them were unpaved dirt lanes: dusty when the weather was dry, quagmires when it rained. During the first decades of car use, drivers routinely packed a small arsenal of tools to carry out roadside repairs.

No national system of roads existed. An abortive bid to create one started when President Thomas Jefferson inveigled Congress into passing the Enabling Act of 1802, which authorized an east–west route from Cumberland, Maryland, to Wheeling, West Virginia—a thoroughfare that would be called the National Road. Subsequent presidents took widely divergent views on whether states or the federal government should pay for such improvements. James Monroe vetoed funds to improve the National Road; his successor, John Quincy Adams, restored the funding. Andrew Jackson opposed all such measures, arguing that states should shoulder the costs. By 1850, the National Road—which by then theoretically extended all the way to Indianapolis—was so degraded that settlers were planting crops and building houses in its right-of-way. The railroads had started winding the countryside in bands of steel, and any thoughts of coordinated road building fell by the wayside. The railroad network grew from about nine thousand track miles in 1850 to nearly two hundred thousand by the turn of the century. America's rail system was world-class, but its road infra-

structure was frequently compared, unfavorably, to those of
barely developed nations.

Even so, there were doughty souls ready to use their primi-
tive automobiles to live out the all-American fantasy of a cross-
country road trip. In 1903, a Vermont physician named
H. Nelson Jackson accepted a bet of fifty dollars to prove that
he could drive from San Francisco to New York. He set out on
May 23 with a hired mechanic, Sewell K. Croker, and a two-
seat open-top Winton purchased on Croker's recommendation.
They arrived in New York on July 26, accompanied by a stray
bulldog they had picked up in Idaho and named Bud. (He was
given his own set of goggles to protect his eyes from road dust.)
Of the sixty-five days it had taken them to cross the six-
thousand-mile route, a total of about three weeks had been
taken up by stops for repairs, rest breaks, and long waits for the
arrival of replacement parts.

Such cross-country feats required a combination of experience, patience, clairvoyance, and simple dumb luck. Local
roads tended to radiate outward from railroad stops, providing
links for farmers to get their produce and stock to market but
offering no direct path for anyone passing through. Even when
roads were improved with gravel, macadam, or wooden planks,
it was not uncommon for such niceties to end abruptly at
county and state lines. It was also not unheard of for a property
owner to put a fence across a road that ran through or along his
land. Litigation over roads and the responsibility for their up-
keep is a major part of the American historical record. Even
when a slightly more orderly system of taxes was created to
fund the maintenance of local roads, the question of which
roads to improve became a political issue, particularly in New
Jersey, where political disputes are the very stuff of life. Whole
towns voted themselves into existence in the late nineteenth

and early twentieth centuries because of disputes over road-maintenance funds and how to use them.

The renewed push for a better system of roads came not from car owners, but from bicyclists. The passion for bicycle riding had grown during the late nineteenth century, and by the 1890s roughly four million Americans owned bicycles. They didn't much like muddy roads, and since bicycling was a pastime of the middle and upper classes, their complaints tended to find sympathetic ears in government. One national cyclists club, the League of American Wheelmen, evolved into a pressure group for road improvements: the name of its in-house publication, *Good Roads*, became the banner for the growing national movement.

The rise of the "Good Roads" movement paralleled interest at the federal level. The year 1893 saw the launch of the Office of Road Inquiry, a precursor to the Federal Highway Administration, which sought to build public support by demonstrating how paved roads could be maintained far more cheaply than unimproved dirt tracks. The first such "object lesson road" was built by the ORI in June 1897, at the entrance to the New Jersey Agricultural College and Experiment Station at New Brunswick, New Jersey (later to become part of Rutgers University). The ORI's man in the field, General E. G. Harrison of Asbury Park, New Jersey, applied six inches of ground traprock, or macadam, to a 660-foot section of the main road running from the city center to the college farm. States followed suit with their own road agencies, goosed along by the Post Office Appropriations Act of 1912, which allocated funds to improve roads for rural free delivery routes, and the Federal Aid Road Act of 1916, which required that states have an official highway department, staffed with qualified engineers, in order to receive federal money for public road projects.

All the while, the role of the automobile continued to expand in America. By 1912, roughly 180,000 registered automobiles were registered in the country. Affiliated industries—service stations and other car-related businesses—were taking shape. Private companies were interested in using motorized trucks to haul goods. It was inevitable that drivers would begin dreaming of a transnational highway.

One such dreamer was Carl Graham Fisher, athlete, entrepreneur, and owner of the Indianapolis Motor Speedway, which he had paved with bricks in 1911 to improve the driving surface for an annual race he dubbed the Indianapolis 500. A man with a nose for publicity stunts and hype—he had once tied a Stoddard-Dayton automobile to a hot-air balloon and lofted it across Indianapolis—Graham enlisted automobile manufacturers in his plan to promote what he called the Coast-to-Coast Rock Highway. Henry Joy, president of the Packard Motor Car Company, and Goodyear president Frank Seiberling pledged money to the project, which Graham hoped to see finished in time for the Pan-American Exposition of 1915. That timetable was scotched when Henry Ford refused to participate—he felt taxpayers would never fund road projects if they thought private industry would carry the burden—but the trio continued to lobby Congress for help in realizing the road, which they dubbed the Lincoln Highway.

By 1913, the route for the Lincoln Highway had been established: beginning in Manhattan's Times Square, it would traverse the country in a more or less straight line through New Jersey, Pennsylvania, Ohio, Indiana, Illinois, Iowa, Nebraska, Wyoming, Utah, Nevada, and California, where it would reach its terminus in San Francisco's Lincoln Park. The plan essentially stitched together a line of existing local roads and proposed links, which the host states would be expected to upgrade with materials provided by the Lincoln Highway Association. Some adjustments had to be made to placate the governors of states, like Colorado, that had pledged support to the grand scheme only to find themselves bypassed by the route. After heavy rounds of lobbying and marketing, the first concrete-paved seedling mile of the Lincoln Highway was completed in DeKalb, Illinois, in the fall of 1914. The next year saw two more in Nebraska, along with separate miles in Illinois and Indiana. The project was finally rolling, spurred by civic booster-ism and the fears of local businesses that traffic would bypass them if the road went unimproved. The U.S. Army got into the act by organizing a transcontinental military convoy for the summer of 1919. The eighty-one vehicles left Washington, D.C., on July 7, joined the Lincoln Highway at Gettysburg, Pennsylvania, and spent the next two months being driven, towed, and frequently pushed toward San Francisco, encountering every conceivable type of road hazard along the way. The heavily publicized tour drew national attention and made a deep impression on a twenty-eight-year-old lieutenant colonel named Dwight D. Eisenhower, who harkened back to his time on the 1919 expedition when he unveiled his vision for a national highway system nearly four decades later.

Highway projects exploded across the country, generating a confusing welter of names, and in 1925 the government instituted a system of numbering for interstate highways. The old Lincoln Highway route, appropriately, was designated Route 1.

The decades spanning the late nineteenth century and the early twentieth century might well be called the heroic age of public works, ushered in by new processes to produce high-quality steel cheaply and in bulk. Steel had long been recognized as both stronger and lighter than iron; a European engineer had used steel as early as 1828, for a suspension bridge across the Danube Canal near Vienna. But the creation of three magnificent steel bridges between 1874 and 1883—James Buchanan Eads's bridge across the Mississippi River at St. Louis; William Sooy Smith's span across the Missouri River at Glasgow, Missouri; and above all the Brooklyn Bridge, designed by John Roebling and completed by his son Washington—ushered in a golden age of bridge building.

New York City was the chief beneficiary of this renaissance. After the Brooklyn Bridge opened with a spectacular ceremony on May 24, 1883, other spans were commissioned to bring automobile traffic directly across the East River: the Williamsburg Bridge (1903), the Manhattan Bridge (1909), and the Queensboro Bridge (1909). (To these would eventually be added the heroically proportioned Triborough Bridge in 1936 and the Throgs Neck Bridge in 1961.) But these merely speeded up transit between Manhattan and its vassal boroughs. Not until the Hells Gate railroad bridge opened in 1916 did bridge-building fever give Manhattan a connection with the mainland through the Bronx. The Hudson River remained a wall separating Manhattan from the road system gradually taking shape across the country. The Hudson and Manhattan Railroad, a light railway connecting Jersey City and lower Manhattan through tunnels beneath the river, had been operating since 1908, but it carried passengers, not freight. A direct connection for cars and trucks was desperately needed.

There was no shortage of plans. The great engineer Gustav Lindenthal proposed a Brobdingnagian span in 1910 that would have combined twelve rail lines with twenty vehicle lanes on two decks, supported by skyscraper-sized towers that would have obliterated several blocks of prime commercial space in midtown Manhattan. The plan, which befuddled the legendary engineer's friends as well as his foes, eventually collapsed under the weight of Lindenthal's ambition. It would be another generation before one of Lindenthal's assistants, Othmar Ammann, realized the design for a bridge across the Hudson.

The clash of interests between the ferry companies, the railroads, and the patronage-obsessed Democratic political machines of Hudson County and New York City was a barrier even more formidable than that presented by the Hudson River and the Meadowlands. Edward I. Edwards, who became governor of New Jersey in 1920 with the backing of the Hudson County machine, twice vetoed legislation to create the nascent Port Authority of New York and New Jersey because his boss, Mayor Frank Hague of Jersey City, feared the new agency would mean the loss of patronage opportunities.

But with ferries carrying upwards of thirty million vehicles across the river each year, something needed to be done. Oceangoing ships docked in New York, but the railroads that carried goods and passengers for shipment stopped at the Jersey bank. The passage across the Hudson River could take a half hour and longer, to which was added the hours needed to offload on the Jersey side, load cargo onto barges and ferries, wait for space to open up at one of the Manhattan piers, then transfer the cargo once again. Waiting trains and railcars frequently backed up all the way across the Meadowlands and beyond.

This is the era when the great railways set the stage for their own obsolescence: though they were beset by rising labor costs and a brief recession that cut into their profits, the rail barons made everything worse by cutting back on rolling stock and practicing false economies. As a result, when export traffic through the railways doubled in the years between 1915 and 1919, antiquated port facilities created immense bottlenecks.

Though the United States did not enter the Great War until 1917, the threat of German submarine attacks wreaked havoc in New York Harbor: sometimes ships remained at dock because their captains were afraid to venture out; often trains would arrive to take cargo from ships that had been sent to the bottom of the Atlantic. Foodstuffs rotted in stalled railroad cars. Cargo was often dumped along the railroad tracks to be gathered up for shipment. While the railroads were destroying themselves, the seeds of the modern trucking industry were being sown as transport companies noted the relative flexibility and reliability of cargo trucks.

Once America entered the conflict, hundreds of thousands of troops began arriving to board ships bound for Europe; the railroads, already undermanned, lost personnel to the draft and found themselves unable to cope with the huge increase in passenger traffic. To top it off, the winter of 1917–18 was unusually severe, with several weeks of heavy snowfall immobilizing vital shipments of supplies. Trains would move ahead a few yards at a time as their crews shoveled snow away from the tracks. Once they arrived, they found the Hudson River clogged with ice and impassable by ferries. The result was a "coal famine" in Manhattan.

That year a joint commission was formed to study the possibilities for a Hudson River crossing from New Jersey into lower Manhattan. The commissioners favored a tunnel, since the low-lying topography did not lend itself to a bridge high enough to allow the passage of ships. And so, in 1919 the commissioners selected Clifford Holland, a Harvard-educated engineer with considerable expertise in tunnel design, to make it happen. Three more years of wrangling were necessary before the tunneling began on October 26, 1922.

·   ·   ·

The amount of labor—physical, mental, and political—that went into the planning, creation, and completion of the tunnel literally boggles the mind.

The brunt of it was borne by the "sandhogs," the workmen who steeled themselves each day to labor under the river. They advanced—sometimes several yards each day, sometimes only a few feet—behind steel shields thirty feet across, with skirts sixteen feet long. (One observer likened them to enormous glass tumblers.) The shields—built along the lines of the "Greathead Shield" used to build London's Tower Subway in 1869—were rammed through the riverbed by pneumatic jacks with a combined thrust of about six thousand tons. As the shields crept forward, sandhogs cleared away slippery muck and rock, then erected a lining of iron rings that gave the tunnels the appearance of monstrous rib cages. The rings were made up of sections that had to be fastened into place with bolts that weighed ten pounds each; tightening one required a pair of men applying their combined weight to a wrench roughly the length of two baseball bats.

The work was hellishly dangerous: the tunnels were pressurized in order to keep river water from flooding the excavation, and the resulting environment was a world unto itself. Fires burned with greater intensity in the oxygen-rich workplace—a lit cigarette reduced itself to ash within moments. Visitors to the tunnels, challenged to whistle, discovered that the air pressure against their lips made it impossible to produce any sound. Workmen entered and left the tunnels through air locks, and the pressure within the tunnels had to be monitored closely at all times. Insufficient pressure would allow water to leach into the tunnels, but too much could produce a blowout—an explosive breach of the tunnel wall that could suck away tools, equipment, and even workmen unlucky

enough to be standing nearby. To prevent this, barges posi-
tioned over the path of the work would dump tons of clay onto
soft areas of the riverbed to provide stability.

Even so, thirty-five workmen had to flee for their lives in
1924 when a shield cut through an unexpectedly soft section of
riverbed and water came gushing through an opening twenty
feet long and two feet wide. Compressed air forced its way up
through the muck and jetted to the surface, where it exploded
in a fifty-foot geyser that scared the daylights out of a boater
but otherwise did no damage.

The longer a man stayed below, the more time he had to
spend in an air lock, where the air pressure around him and
within his body would gradually be reduced to that of sea level.
Walking into the open air without proper adjustment resulted
in crippling decompression sickness, or "the bends"—agoniz-
ing, sometimes fatal cramps produced by nitrogen bubbles
formed within the bloodstream by the abrupt change in pressure.

"Think twice, you only live once" was and is the maxim of
every sandhog working underground. Even so, fifteen men
died during work on the project. Though Holland's easygoing
poise and readiness to get his hands dirty earned him the re-
spect of the sandhogs, the crews went out on strike several
times to demand more pay, shorter working hours, and reduced
air pressure.

Up at ground level, the environment was no less pressurized.
Before Holland could proceed with his iron-based tunnel design, he had to do battle with the great George Washington
Goethals, the army officer who ascended to near godhood
when he guided the Panama Canal project to completion in
1914. Upon his retirement from the military in 1916, Goethals
set himself up as a consulting engineer in New York and as-

sumed a major role in advising the design of the transportation
network taking shape around the city. For the trans-Hudson
traffic tunnel, Goethals favored a masonry tunnel design, arguing that it could be completed faster and more cheaply than
an iron tunnel. The Goethals plan would also have employed a
construction method patented by John F. O'Rourke, a Tam-
many-connected engineer who would profit handsomely from
royalties if the Goethals design was used. Holland had to
demonstrate repeatedly that a masonry tunnel would literally
become buoyant in the fluid silt at the bottom of the Hudson
River.

Even with Goethals defeated, Holland had to endure the
headaches generated from the New York side by Tammany
Hall and, from the Jersey side, by the Hudson County machine. Owners of Jersey City properties that would be razed for
approaches to the tunnel—quite often shell companies with a
provenance that led back to City Hall and Frank Hague's office, as local legend had it—would demand Park Avenue prices
for their run-down tenements; if the state seized the property,
the owners would contest the payments and, under orders of a
Hague-connected judge, win vastly inflated prices.

Virtually every detail, even the choice of draftsmen to
prepare blueprints, involved arguments and grandstanding
among the New York and the New Jersey commissioners. The
official groundbreaking on the New York side took place on
March 31, 1922, but groundbreaking on the New Jersey side
was delayed for two months. The western end of the project
required the use of land owned by the Erie Railroad, and con-
cessions had to be worked out. Then the New Jersey commissioners demanded agreements on street improvements, with
work to be carried out by politically connected contractors.

An agreement was finally reached with the New Jersey

commissioners in mid-May, but one last delay loomed—they wanted to hold a gala groundbreaking ceremony on July 4. This was too much even for a man of Holland's nearly Olympian patience. On May 31, Holland slipped into the Erie rail yard to hold a clandestine groundbreaking with R. C. Falconer, chief engineer of the Erie Railroad, and George H. Flinn, one of the principal contractors. It must have been no small satisfaction for Holland to feel the shovel's blade cut into the dirt, even if he might have preferred to use it on the necks of any or all of the New Jersey commissioners.

This groundbreaking made it more difficult for the commissioners to delay work any longer, though they continued to plague Holland with new demands. At one point, the New Jersey commissioners had even wanted to see themselves commemorated with a twenty-foot granite pillar and a bronze plaque bearing their faces, to be placed in the New Jersey toll plaza. "Nothing that the New York Commissioners have done compares with the celerity with which they rejected the idea," the *New York Times* reported, noting that "one of them tartly suggested that the name and face of the Commissioner who originated the idea should be done in brass and not in bronze."

Hudson County's point man, and the lone Democratic appointee among the New Jersey commissioners, was John F. Boyle, a banker, real estate investor, and financial adviser to Frank Hague. He was also the owner of Boyle's Thirty Acres, the Jersey City arena venerated by boxing fans as the place where Jack Dempsey defeated Georges Carpentier in 1921. Surrounded by Republican appointees, Boyle proved to be Dempsey's equal as a verbal pugilist, generating a steady stream of complaints about the slights and injustices New Jersey and Jersey City had to endure at the hands of the New York tunnel commissioners. When Holland staged his clandestine groundbreaking, Boyle exploded at the next commission meeting. "I don't see why a great project like this was started in such a contemptible and sneaky manner!" he raged. Six years after his death in 1930, Jersey City paid tribute to Boyle's relentless pettifogging by designating a grid of streets on the Holland Tunnel approach "Boyle Plaza." What was true then is equally true now—there's no getting to the tunnel without first going through John Boyle.

Holland had spent some eighteen years working on various underground projects, and years of shuttling between the bizarre environment of the caissons and the equally pressurized world of politics steadily eroded his mental and physical health. Aboveground, every move demanded scores of negotiations and strategies. Belowground, the tunneling work required constant recalibration to ensure that the excavation crews closing in from opposite sides of the river would actually meet; if the slightest deviation was detected, a day of work would be lost while the pneumatic jacks were adjusted to keep the shields moving along the plotted course. Even then, Holland's doubts would not be put to rest until the workmen actually holed through.

The endless stress finally got the better of Holland, and in the summer of 1924 he suffered a nervous breakdown. He was immediately granted a three-month paid leave, which he was to spend recuperating at Dr. John Harvey Kellogg's famous sanitarium in Battle Creek, Michigan. After apparently regaining some of his health, Holland suffered a heart attack and died two days before the first work crew holed through the muck beneath the Hudson River. The signal that set off the explosion was triggered by Holland's second in command, acting chief engineer Milton Freeman. Freeman himself died of pneumonia brought on by overwork only four months after as-

The New York and New Jersey commissioners overseeing the Holland Tunnel project posed for this photograph during an August 21, 1926, inspection tour of the passage. New York governor Al Smith reaches across the boundary to shake hands with New Jersey governor A. Harry Moore. At the extreme right, Jersey City Mayor Frank Hague (bisected by the edge of the photograph) glowers at the camera while Commissioner John Boyle, Hague's man on the Holland Tunnel project, aims his trademark bulldog glare at the camera.

suming control. Ole Singstad, third in the chain of command, oversaw the completion of the tunnel, which was named in honor of Clifford Holland.

But even if Holland had lived to see the completion of the tunnel, it is possible that the thought of sharing credit with the politicians who had made his life hell would have felled him on the spot. They can be seen in that famous handshake photo, arrayed on either side of the New York–New Jersey boundary. The most crucial one is the fourth man standing behind A. Harry Moore.

He is on the extreme right of the photo, almost cropped out completely. Typically, Frank Hague is still wearing his hat, and instead of smiling he is regarding his surroundings with his usual baleful glare. The photograph has been reproduced many times in magazines and newspapers, and often Hague is missing.

In the great tale of the construction of the Holland Tunnel, Jersey City mayor Frank Hague was only a background figure. But another traffic project was on the way—one that would put him front and center.

CHAPTER 2

The Horseshoe
Against the World

For those who don't remember him, Frank Hague was a combination of Boss Tweed and Carlo Gambino. He ran Jersey City and the state of New Jersey from 1917 to 1949. If you objected to the way he ordered the body politic, the safest thing to do was leave the state—and probably the country.

> —Thomas Fleming, historian, Jersey City native

[Hague] was almost a demigod to the people of Jersey City and Hudson County, and only slightly smaller in rank to the Democratic party of the state of New Jersey and the nation. . . . The only fights he ever lost were those he secretly chose to lose, and then only because he had sewed up the opposition so that, in effect, they too were working for him.

> —LeRoy E. McWilliams, pastor, St. Michael's Parish

On a typical workday in the first decade of the twenty-first century, thousands of eastbound drivers stream through Jersey City on their way to the Holland Tunnel, whether by the Pulaski Skyway, the Newark Bay Extension of the New Jersey Turnpike, or the elaborate, truck-clogged twists and turns of

Route 1-9, which nuzzle the supports of the Skyway like an affectionate cat.

The descent to the Holland Tunnel toll plaza takes drivers past the huge redbrick mass of the old Seaboard Terminal building and expansive gas stations. Until recently, what passed for a Jersey City skyline registered chiefly as the foothills of the mountainous offices of lower Manhattan, with only the Newport Centre residential high-rise (constructed during the 1980s) staking any kind of claim to visibility. Thanks to the office diaspora that followed the destruction of the World Trade Center, Jersey City has begun to acquire its own wall of office towers along the Hudson River waterfront, with the Goldman Sachs and J. P. Morgan Chase buildings showing the way.

As the drivers reach the Holland Tunnel toll plaza, it's unlikely that any of them think about the teeming slum neighborhood that once steamed and smoldered there. Even fewer, it is certain, realize that the ground beneath their wheels was once a maze of narrow streets and neighborhoods with names like Cork Row. They are driving over the birthplace of Frank Hague, and if any one of them has the impulse to smirk about it, he ought to bear in mind that at one time there would have been plenty of people ready to wipe the smile off his face. For most of the first half of the twentieth century, Jersey City was "Hagueville," and Hague was its master. To his numerous critics, Hague was "the Hudson County Hitler," an American dictator whose regime looted city coffers and whose critics risked everything from punitive tax assessments on their property to false arrests and vicious beatings at the hands of the city's legendarily brutal police force. To his less numerous supporters, Hague was "Duh Mare," the man who kept food on their tables, coal in their cellars, and roofs over their heads during the bleakest years of the Depression.

Though Hague has been judged too harshly in many ways, he has gotten off too easily in others. The reeking slum along this route is where Hague's story began; the bright concrete lanes that replaced it opened the way to the battles of the Skyway; together, they set the stage for the ugliest incident of Hague's career, and marked his transformation into the kind of ruler his critics had always accused him of being.

For much of its history, Jersey City has been a place that people traveled *through* rather than *to*. Because of its position across the Hudson River from the lowest and most accessible portion of Manhattan, the city has been the terminus for just about every form of transportation technology used in a given period: stagecoaches and ferries in the eighteenth century; railroads in the nineteenth and early twentieth centuries; highways from the twentieth century to the present. Newark, its sister city across the Meadowlands, may have gotten the airport, but Jersey City got everything else. Even the Morris Canal, that engineering marvel that brought goods all the way from Phillipsburg on the other side of the state, had its terminus in Jersey City. It was an achievement for its builders, an asset for its customers, and an affliction for its host city, which was all but cut off from its southern portion by the new waterway.

The canal wasn't the only man-made barrier. The Pennsylvania, Erie, DL&W, Central, and Lehigh Valley railroad lines all cut through the city at various points. Clanking, steaming lines of boxcars and engines at street level formed mobile barriers that could turn streets into cul-de-sacs without warning. The street grid of Jersey City was already a hodgepodge—a legacy of the 1869 merger of Jersey City with the neighboring communities of Bergen and Hudson City—and the rail lines only made it worse.

A few blocks south of what would become the Holland Tunnel entrance, residents of the Hamilton Park and Harsimus Cove neighborhoods had to endure a looming trestle of timber and iron that carried Pennsylvania Railroad trains from an open cut—a man-made gap blasted through Bergen Hill—to and from the Harsimus Yards on the waterfront, morning, noon, and night. The trestle was replaced in 1905 with "the Embankment"—a twenty-seven-foot-high Maginot Line of sandstone and granite that ran for six blocks between Fifth and Sixth streets.

Perhaps the unkindest cut of all came when the Erie Railroad, the most luxurious and reliable passenger line of its day, decided to replace its narrow, smoke-filled train tunnel through Bergen Hill with something better. In 1906, an army of workmen began the four-year task of blasting, digging, and carving an eighty-five-foot-deep canyon through Jersey City that would be wide enough to give passage to four separate rail lines. The creation of the mile-long "Erie Cut" involved engineering on a pharaonic scale: 160,000 cubic yards of earth were removed, and 250,000 pounds of dynamite were used to blast away 800,000 cubic yards of traprock. The project was preceded by years of litigation with city property owners; several blocks of houses and even a church were either demolished or physically moved from the path of the construction. Once the work began, homeowners along the periphery of the site would find chunks of rock littering their gardens and sidewalks—construction debris hurled from the trench by dynamite explosions. From time to time, a particularly robust detonation would send a good-sized boulder arcing through the sky to crash through someone's roof.

The Erie Cut became operational on June 13, 1910. Dignitaries and Jersey City residents gathered to peer down into the gaping trench as the first trains emerged from the mouth of the tunnel entrance to the west, roared between the looming rock walls on either side, and began the descent to the waterfront along an immense trestle. No longer would coal smoke from train engines choke passengers as they were carried through the Bergen Tunnel; now it would merely billow up from the Erie Cut and soil the walls and windows of Jersey City householders.

Running along the top of the cut were lines of flowerbeds and wrought-iron fencing, ornaments graciously installed by the railroad. A few local streets spanned the gully, supported by arches of traprock—the "Bergen Arches"—but the fact remained that Jersey City was now split by a hissing, seething, roaring man-made crevasse, sixty feet wide at the base and one hundred feet wide at the top, billowing with cinders and coal smoke. The railroads brought jobs with them, but once again Jersey City was simply a staging area for passengers bound for the Manhattan ferries, or New Yorkers making weekend excursions to "the country"—northern New Jersey—and points west.

The impact of the railroads on Jersey City was not merely physical. Railroad interests pulled the strings in Trenton, and the Republican-dominated state legislature allowed them to use their land essentially tax-free, denying the city a major source of revenue. Railroads controlled virtually all of the Jersey City waterfront. The railroads even played a part in what is thus far the worst disaster to strike Jersey City: the July 30,

1916, explosion at Black Tom Island, a depot at the end of a mile-long pier maintained by the Lehigh Valley Railroad. The warehouses on the island were packed with war materiel for shipment to the battle lines in Europe. Shortly after two in the morning, a series of cataclysmic explosions ripped through the depot with enough force to shatter windows in lower Manhattan and leave chunks of shrapnel embedded in the copper skin of the Statue of Liberty. Jersey City residents walked through streets sown with shattered glass and gazed at the *Jersey Journal* building, where the big clock had been impaled by flying debris, stopping it at 2:12 a.m. Though the explosion was the result of German sabotage, an inquiry found that both the Lehigh Valley and Central railroads had violated time limits on the storage of munitions at the depot. No penalties or sanctions against the railroads followed.

In Jersey City, social caste was expressed through topography. The Protestant elite occupied "the Heights," the area atop Bergen Hill, and they never missed an opportunity to grind their heels into lower-class, Irish American faces. The city they ruled was a place where many factories posted signs warning: "NO CATHOLICS NEED APPLY." Applicants could show up day after day at the hiring office and be asked: "Catholic or Protestant?" Any man willing to say "Protestant," even if everyone in the crowd knew otherwise, would finally get a job. The anti-Irish prejudice was reflected in the wider society: terms like "paddy wagon" were part of the popular lexicon, newspaper illustrators (including the lauded cartoonist and crusader Thomas Nast) routinely depicted Irish people with simian features, and deep thinkers of the era regularly argued that the Irish would never be able to assimilate successfully into mainstream society. The prejudice produced among the immigrants and their children a bottomless well of rage that burned across generations.

In the mid-nineteenth century, New Jersey was still largely a rural state with only two cities of any appreciable size: Jersey City and Newark. Appalled by the masses of immigrants flooding into the cities, and leery of the influence of the Democratic Party among these uncouth, unwashed, and Catholic hordes, the Republican elites running Trenton used the 1869 consolidation of Jersey City with neighboring towns in order to dilute Democratic power, then crafted the new city charter that followed the merger to carve Jersey City into six wards, with the growing Democratic element—heavily Irish and Italian, and mostly Catholic—isolated within the second ward. The oddly shaped district quickly became known as the Horseshoe, sometimes shortened to the 'Shoe.

It was a grindingly poor area, jammed with shanties, squatter shacks, and wooden tenements jammed shoulder to shoulder. Its inhabitants were Irish and German immigrants who worked on the docks or in the rail yards, poaching coal from the train cars to heat their homes. Livestock—chickens and pigs—often shared space in the crowded houses. Streets were covered with sheets of water after rainstorms. There were some forty saloons—virtually one on every corner—and drunken brawls were a common sight. Children grew up fighting, and learned early that membership in a local gang was the only guarantee of safety. Waves of typhoid would sweep through the neighborhoods, leaving funerals in their wake.

The area was layered with smells: the earthy stink of horse dung from the streets; the sour reek of rotting garbage from the waterfront, where the Central Railroad of New Jersey was landfilling refuse from New York City in order to extend its land holdings along the Jersey City waterfront; and the nauseating stench of boiling fat from the vats of the Colgate soap plant a little ways south in Paulus Hook. Palls of acrid smoke from factory chimneys darkened buildings. The air was also full of sound. Tugboat whistles could be heard from the bay and the mouth of the Hudson River. Horse-drawn carts pounded along the cobblestone streets; overriding them was the screech and clatter of trains moving back and forth at street level.

Politics was a full-contact sport, played with great ruthlessness and an eye to the main chance. Elections were occasions for brawls that often metastasized into riots. Ward bosses and their lieutenants worked constantly to get out the vote, and sent thugs to beat up members of the opposition on the way to the polling places. "Floaters" were hired to travel from one polling place to the next, casting as many votes as possible for designated candidates. Ballot boxes were usually jammed with as many additional paper ballots as needed to ensure the proper outcome. In 1889, no fewer than sixty-five Irish Americans were convicted of stuffing some ten thousand ballots into voting boxes, only to be pardoned by the governor, Leon Abbett— a Jersey City native.

The Horseshoe was to Frank Hague—born there on January 17, 1876—what the West Bottoms section of Kansas City was to Jim and Tom Pendergast, or the Back of the Yards area of Chicago was to Richard J. Daley—an incubator, a home base, and a training ground for using the mechanisms of political power.

History records that Frank Hague was ushered into Democratic political life in 1896 by Ned Kenny, a tavern owner known as "the mayor of Cork Row," the section of the Horseshoe where Hague was born. In another two decades it would be razed for the approach to the Holland Tunnel.

Kenny was worried about business and political pressures from a rival saloon owner, Denny McLaughlin, who was a lieutenant for Robert "Little Bob" Davis, the Democratic boss of the Second Ward. McLaughlin was a formidable opponent: he owned tenements throughout the city and in Hoboken, as well as a piece of a racetrack in Guttenberg, just to the north. He had opened a new bar, the Park House, to cut into Kenny's business. There would soon be a special election for constables (a sort of neighborhood police official), and he needed allies to protect his flank.

At the age of twenty, Hague was already cutting an impressive figure in the Horseshoe. His father, John Hague, who worked first as a blacksmith for the Erie Railroad and then as a guard for the Beehive Bank, was a man with eight children to feed and not much time to keep an eye on them. His mother, Margaret, was by all accounts the more forceful of the couple—one old-timer recalled her years later as "a bitch on wheels." Hague's younger brother, Jimmy, never quite escaped from her orbit and would always be known as a mama's boy.

Young Frank Hague, the fourth oldest in the family, had been expelled from the sixth grade for habitual truancy. He and two brothers, John and Hugh, had run with a gang called the Red Tigers, brawling with lace-curtain Irish kids from Hamilton Park, swiping goods from local merchants, stealing coal and brass fixtures from locomotives waiting for the ferry to New York, and doing favors for local political players.

A few odd jobs—including a brief stint as a blacksmith's helper for the Erie rail line, at a salary of a dollar a day—had given Frank Hague all the experience he wanted of honest labor. As a teenager, Hague had tried boxing, then reinvented himself as a manager of a Brooklyn lightweight named Joseph Craig. Craig went nowhere as a boxer, but Hague used the income to acquire his first natty suits. Witnesses describe him stalking around the Horseshoe in four-button, double-breasted plaid suits with a cape fashionably slung over the left shoulder. Tall and athletic-looking, with red hair already thinning out and ice-blue eyes that could flash with anger, Hague dressed like a swell and carried himself like a man who could not be trifled with. In conversation he would use his height to over-awe the other man; he would emphasize points with a jabbing index finger, as though trying to write his message in bruises across the other man's chest. Though capable of applying charm, he was quick with his fists—a habit that stayed with him throughout his life. Yet, while Hague never shrank from a scuffle, he early on showed an aptitude for getting others to do his fighting for him.

It didn't take long for Kenny to convince Hague that politics would be a good career path. Hague requested seventy-five dollars "to make friends," and Kenny pulled the funds from a cigar box under the bar. That amount of money could buy a lot of friends in 1896, and Hague polled 1,571 votes to the 560 garnered by his opponent in the spring election.

As the next election approached, freshly minted Constable Frank Hague established himself as a superb campaigner eager to ring doorbells and get out the vote. The presidential election of 1896 gave the Republicans control of the White House for the next sixteen years: Democratic candidate William Jennings Bryan, who had brought the nominating convention to its feet with his "Cross of Gold" speech, was crushed by GOP candidate William McKinley in a national sweep that included Jersey City. But the Democrats won two crucial municipal seats, sheriff and county surrogate, thanks to a huge showing in the Second Ward. Hague's role in securing that vote was noted by Davis and others. Hague was on his way up in the city's Democratic organization.

Political machines came about for the same reason political parties sprang into being—they were necessary. Multiple waves of immigrants were arriving in American cities, and they were expected to make their way with no governmental help. By trading basic community services for unswerving loyalty on election day, machines performed a much needed function.

For this reason, Frank Hague's life as a foot soldier for the Democratic organization was not an easy one. To show residents of his territory that the Democratic Party was their friend, Hague was on call twenty-four hours a day: to plunk down bail money for a family member arrested on a petty charge; to transport a sick child to the hospital; to find new lodging for a family rendered homeless by a fire; to arrange coal deliveries in the winter. When new residents arrived, Hague was expected to lead them through the cumbersome and confusing process of registering to vote.

Hague and his fellows were not given to writing things down. Fortunately for students of politics, across the river in Manhattan a Tammany Hall operative named George Washington Plunkitt started using a bootblack stand outside the New York County Court House as an informal office. During the last decade of the nineteenth century, Plunkitt's advice and observations about life in the Tammany political machine were taken down by a *New York Evening Post* reporter. Published as a slender book in 1905, Plunkitt's stories about the daily workings of the Tammany machine offer glimpses into a career that was lucrative but never leisurely:

What tells in holdin' your grip on your district is to go right down among the poor families and help them in the different ways they need help. I've got a regular system for this. If there's a fire in Ninth, Tenth or Eleventh Avenue, for example, any hour of the day or night, I'm usually there with some of my election district captains as soon as the fire engines. If a family is burned out, I don't ask whether they are Republicans or Democrats, and I don't refer them to the Charity Organization Society, which would investigate their case in a month or two and decide they were worthy of help about the time they are dead from starvation. I just get quarters for them, buy clothes for them if their clothes were burned up, and fix them up till they get things runnin' again. It's philanthropy, but it's politics, too—mighty good politics. Who can tell how many votes one of these fires brings me? The poor are the most grateful people in the world, and, let me tell you, they have more friends in their neighborhoods than the rich have in theirs.

Hague, like other party functionaries, also took the lead in arranging parades, picnic excursions, dances, and other social events in a community where recreational opportunities were scarce or nonexistent. Politics was always part of the entertainment menu. Picnics included speeches by local officials; torchlit parades offered a touch of drama and built group loyalties.

It was also the ward operative's goal to establish a personal network of supporters within the larger group of party members. As he rose through the ranks, Hague proved exceptionally shrewd at cultivating advantageous relationships and turning apparent setbacks into fresh opportunities. The first and most striking example came in the fall of 1904. One of his old gang-mates, a childhood friend named Red Dugan, had grown into a small-time criminal who reconciled his career path with his religion by preying mostly on Protestant clergymen. Dugan was arrested for trying to pass a bad check in Roxbury, Massachusetts. Hague and another friend, Thomas Maddigan, decided to go to Boston to testify on Dugan's behalf. Dugan's defense was that he had actually been in Jersey City at the time the check was supposedly passed; Hague and Maddigan would back him up under oath. The fact that Hague had already been subpoenaed to testify in Jersey City on another matter and would miss his court appointment was only a trifling detail.

Hague and Maddigan convinced no one with their testimony, and Red Dugan only made matters worse by confessing to the crime. Dugan was packed off to jail, and Hague returned home to learn that he had been found in contempt of court for skipping the Jersey City hearing. He was fined one hundred dollars and stripped of his deputy sheriff title.

Yet even here, Hague's instincts proved correct. Residents of the Second Ward were suspicious of the police and tended to view the law as a hindrance, not a help. "Contempt of court" was not the sort of thing that bothered the Horseshoe, which showed contempt for the law on a daily basis. But showing loyalty to a friend—that was something the Horseshoe could understand, and applaud. As Denny McLaughlin liked to say, "It's the Horseshoe against the world." And when Hague said he'd done it all at the request of Dugan's mother, all was forgiven among the people who counted most: the voters.

Political machines like the Hudson County operation are commonly described as engines of corruption, but the quid pro quo mind-set of the political bosses seems downright quaint when compared with the governmental and business ethics that prevailed in the post–Civil War era. In 1875, treasury agents exposed a cabal of mostly Republican politicians who had conspired with whiskey distilleries, distributors, and government agents to steal millions of dollars in tax revenues from liquor sales. Before that, financier Jay Gould and his allies had roiled the national economy by flooding the stock market with illegal shares in a bid to take over the Erie Railroad. A financial panic in 1873 toppled twenty banks, erasing the life savings of thousands of depositors. The depredations of tycoons like J. P. Morgan, Andrew Carnegie, and Daniel Drew—men who used their stupendous wealth to crush competitors and buy legislators—eventually led Matthew Josephson to resurrect the medieval epithet "robber barons" for a muckraking book of the same name. The loot-and-plunder culture reached the uppermost levels of government. If nothing else, urban political machines democratized the looting and brought its benefits to those whose forebears had had the bad taste to arrive in America a generation or so later than others. When the Progressive movement put society through spasms of reform, often the motivation was not so much to stop graft as to ensure that it did not fall into the wrong—i.e., immigrant—hands.

Ironically, Frank Hague—the man who would eventually be painted as one of the worst of the machine politicians—added to his power by riding those waves of reform. During the first decade of the twentieth century, Jersey City saw the rise of two reformers. The first, an undertaker named Mark Fagan, scored a number of crippling election victories against "Little Bob" Davis and his organization, creating opportunities for an ambitious rival like Hague. The second, a German grocer named H. Otto Wittpenn, benefited from Hague's support and rewarded him with a cushy job (chief custodian of City Hall) that offered plenty of patronage opportunities. But Hague's biggest boost came from passage of the Walsh Act of 1911, a pet project of Woodrow Wilson, who had graduated from the academic politics of Princeton University to become governor of New Jersey in 1910. The Walsh Act allowed municipalities to revamp their governments into nonpartisan commissions, with each commissioner assigned specific tasks within government. Proponents of the Walsh Act believed that by eliminating the byzantine bureaucracies of cities and establishing clear lines of accountability, voters would have the tools they needed to remove unproductive or corrupt officials.

Jersey City's first commission election put Hague in control of the city police department, and what happened next would have gladdened the heart of any reformer. Under "Little Bob" Davis, Jersey City had been the East Coast equivalent of a brawling Wild West city, and the police were only slightly less frightening than the criminals. Hague immediately set to work dismissing lazy and corrupt police officers, replacing them with tough Horseshoe recruits. In his first display of the concern for detail and hands-on management that would make his political machine legendary, Hague cruised the streets of Jersey City checking up on his men. More than one out-of-shape cop found himself confronted by the menacing Horseshoe brawler, who would order him to report back to the chief and "tell him Commissioner Hague don't want cream puffs like you on the street." Hague earned the favor of church leaders by cracking down on prostitution and narcotics trafficking. His suppression of vice extended to the city's vaudeville theaters, where on more than one occasion a girlie show would be brought to a halt by a police raid, with Commissioner Hague himself stomping across the stage to direct operations.

More ominously, Hague also established an inner circle of elite patrolmen who would spy on the other officers and help him keep the entire force in line. Nicknamed "zeppelins," "zepps" for short, they would grow into a praetorian guard that punished Hague's political opponents as well as recalcitrant cops.

Though he was implacable in going after prostitutes and drug dealers, Hague turned a blind eye to gambling parlors—gambling was closely woven into the fabric of Jersey City life, and betting shops were a ready source of bribe money. The streets of the city undeniably became safer under Hague's stewardship, a fact that won him the support of religious leaders. Even the Republican-owned *Jersey Journal* hailed him as a reformer, and by the 1916 gubernatorial election, Hague's influence in Hudson County had grown so strong that he was able to undermine Wittpenn's bid for the governor's seat.

In a macabre twist, Hague's chances were boosted even further by the murder of Frank Kenny, the son of Ned Kenny—the man whose cigar box of cash had funded Hague's start in politics. Frank Kenny was shot to death on Good Friday during a fight with an Italian man who apparently made an inappropriate remark to Kenny's wife. The killer fled, but Hague and his officers identified the culprit as a steelworker named Michael Rombolo, whom they found holed up in Newark. According to the legend, Rombolo managed to evade the Newark police, only to be run to ground by Hague, who personally drove him back across the Meadowlands to Jersey City.

When Hague arrived with the suspect, he called in John V. Kenny, younger brother of the slain man, and offered him a chance to administer some punishment of his own. Kenny declined, but Hague took the opportunity to kick in a few of Rombolo's ribs. The younger Kenny would remain a loyal offi-

Frank Hague, mayor of Jersey City and boss of a political machine with national clout, was always impeccably tailored. *(Courtesy of the Newark Public Library)*

cer in the Hague machine until 1949, when he turned and gave Hague himself a few kicks to the ribs—figuratively speaking. But that day was still far off.

The city election of 1917 would later be seen as the death of the Progressive movement in New Jersey, though few realized it at the time since talk of reform was still thick in the air. Hague ran as part of a five-man ticket that included A. Harry Moore, a former Wittpenn man now firmly in Hague's camp. Fagan and Wittpenn were swamped, and Hague found himself at the threshold of power over Jersey City.

The commission structure of government required that the mayor's job be given to the top vote getter, which was A. Harry Moore. Instead, Moore graciously offered the reins of authority to Hague, who just as graciously accepted them. They would remain in his hands for the next thirty-two years as

Frank Hague set about making his mark, first on Jersey City and Hudson County, then on New Jersey state politics, and eventually on the White House. But first there were some battles to be fought, particularly with the railroads, as well as some allies to win and some enemies to destroy.

CHAPTER 3

The Slanted Road

Bridges define the approaches to cities, and passing over or under some of the world's great spans is an unforgettable experience. . . . [E]very bridge, small or large, is also an aesthetic and environmental statement. Its lines are important beyond its span; every bridge must not only bear its burden, whether cows or coal trains, but must also be able to withstand the burden of proof that, in the final analysis, society is better served, tangibly and intangibly, by the bridge's being there at all.

—Henry Petroski, *Engineers of Dreams*

The problem of main highway construction and location, therefore, is not one for abutting property owners along the route to solve for their own individual needs, but is one to be solved for state-wide and nation-wide travelers. So also the abettors do not pay for the improvement, but this is paid for by the state or nation at large and its benefits are state-wide and often nation-wide, leading to state-wide and nation-wide developments.

—Fred Lavis, "Economic Theory of Highway Location" (1927)

It's hard to warm up to the Pulaski Skyway. Its imposing black steel mass seems brutal and ugly when compared with the graceful, swooping lines of a suspension design like the George

Washington Bridge. The roadway's spans across the Hackensack and Passaic rivers are truss bridges: where suspension and
cable-stayed bridges seem to spin poetry out of air and steel,
truss bridges look like jumbles of steel beams—all science and
no art. "A truss bridge rarely looks aesthetically pleasing,"
warns *Design of Highway Bridges,* one of the field's basic
texts. Add to that the fact that it crosses some of the most infer-
nally blighted real estate on the eastern seaboard, and many
viewers are left with the impression that this is a structure only
its engineers could love.

And yet, when viewed from a distance that allows it to be
taken in whole, the Skyway looks curiously graceful. It rises
from the swamp on a series of huge concrete piers that were
once gleaming white but are now grimed by seven decades of
weather and traffic exhaust. The elevated highway, or viaduct,
seems to float above the piers; its bottom chords arch from pier
to pier, as though the behemoth were standing *en pointe* all the
way across the Meadowlands. The effect is particularly striking
when the elevated highway rises to meet the bridges spanning
the Hackensack and Passaic rivers, and the top chords—which
are set roughly at shoulder height along the roadway—vault
upward to form two points atop each span, then flow down to
rejoin the viaduct. Between the chords, a lattice of K-shaped
trusses adds strength, rigidity, and the sense that we are looking at a survivor from the Industrial Revolution instead of a
Depression-era highway project.

In his comprehensive work *American Building Art: The
Twentieth Century,* Carl W. Condit lays out the engineering ar-
gument for celebrating the Skyway:

> Most of the 16,000-foot length of the viaduct is made up
> of short deck-truss cantilever spans, but the crossings of

the Passaic and Hackensack rivers are remarkable examples of swinging trusses of a highly refined and graceful form. The bridges are identical: the river span, of subdivided Pratt trusses, is 550 feet in clear length, with a 75-foot cantilever at each end, and the swinging anchor spans, composed of Pratt trusses of basic form, are each 350 feet long. The whole 1,250-foot length constitutes a continuous unit between the two series of approach spans. . . . The ugly cantilever was at last turned into a structural form that rivaled the graceful and dynamic quality of the steel arch.

When the Federal Writers Project published its guidebook to New Jersey during the last years of the Depression, it used the Skyway as one of the first images to define the Garden State. Because it is part of a historic district corridor linked to the Holland Tunnel, the Skyway, by virtue of the number of cars that cross it each day, can rank among the most-visited and least-loved historic landmarks in America. Unlike the George Washington Bridge, the construction of which overlapped with the Meadowlands project, the Skyway has not inspired well-known music or poetry. Like the Meadowlands it crosses, the Skyway's place in American culture is a junkyard collection of references and tossed-off images.

The viaduct made its first and still most significant contribution to popular culture in 1938, when Orson Welles and the Mercury Theatre staged their famous Halloween radio adaptation of *The War of the Worlds:* the script noted that one of the Martian war machines was straddling the Skyway, giving already frightened listeners the terrifying image of a tripod standing 150 feet above the marshes, ready to incinerate approaching drivers. Five years later, Alfred Hitchcock opened his film *Shadow of a Doubt* with a long shot of the Skyway crossing the still largely pristine Meadowlands, along the way immortalizing two hoboes eating sandwiches on a Hackensack River pier. Over the next few decades, the Skyway was mainly celebrated (with varying degrees of irony) in the songs of local musicians. It was not until the turn of the century that the viaduct was featured in a worthy successor to Hitchcock and Welles: the long-running television series *The Sopranos,* which features the Skyway in its opening credits as mob boss Tony Soprano makes his rounds through Hudson and Essex counties.

So—the Skyway's three major pop culture appearances to date are all associated in some way with either crime or fear. As it turns out, this is not at all inappropriate. The crime aspect will be examined soon enough; for now, fear is the proper starting point.

For drivers leaving Manhattan to begin the Skyway tour—and this is a trip for drivers only: no pedestrians allowed—it all begins with the first glimpse of daylight while rounding the gleaming, tiled curve at the western end of the Holland Tunnel. The driver emerges into a realm of expansive gas stations and boxy warehouses, which he dare not study for more than a few seconds because experienced drivers are already crisscrossing his path, jockeying for position across the five lanes of traffic as it begins the climb to Bergen Hill. For engineering purposes, this stretch—about a third of a mile, from the mouth of the Holland Tunnel—is called the Twelfth Street Viaduct. For sociological purposes, this stretch helps maintain New Jersey's reputation as a Hobbesian wilderness recast in asphalt—a wasteland of automotive bullies, where every car trip is nasty, brutal, and long.

Hurtling westward, the driver must cut to the left. Too far to the right, he will be caught in the flow onto the Turnpike Extension; even lingering in the third or fourth lane carries the risk of being channeled up the center ramp and onto State Highway, and Jersey City's sclerotic network of traffic-clogged local streets. The last chance to choose comes at the Jersey Avenue intersection, between the huge white box occupied by the Port Authority in the wake of the 9/11 terror attacks, and a low-rise housing project called Holland Gardens. Here the driver can either bail out to the left, or hit the gas and surge forward, leaving his fate to the gods of physics.

If all goes well, the driver hits the steep ramp rising from Jersey Avenue and follows the curving road sharply left, keeping a wary eye on the lanes to his immediate right, where other drivers are trying to bull their way through by sheer intimidation. The two lanes then cut sharply to the right, and the driver enters a tunnel with high concrete walls, just wide enough for the two lanes of traffic. The correct name for this is the Hoboken Avenue Viaduct, but engineers often call it "the depressed roadway"—one of those accidentally poetic technical terms the scientific world occasional yields up, like "cloud chamber" or "hopeful monsters."

Most civic engineers consider this 3,380-foot-long stretch the most interesting and innovative portion of the route. By blasting a 28-foot-deep cut through Bergen Hill, then roofing it over with a brand-new road called State Highway, the Skyway's engineers minimized the new highway's impact on Jersey City's local streets. Compared to the multiple indignities inflicted by the railroads, which made rational traffic planning all but impossible, or the corridor of blight created decades later by the New Jersey Turnpike's Newark Bay Extension, this is no small thing. The southern edge of the cut is open to the air; this, combined with grillwork along State Highway, eliminates the need for artificial ventilation. It also allows drivers, stalled in one of the route's frequent traffic jams, the chance to study what amounts to a diorama of Bergen Hill's geological foundation.

Emerging from the tunnel, the driver passes beneath the overpass for JFK Boulevard and crosses into the realm of big engineering. Beneath his tires, lines of Pratt trusses supported by brawny concrete piers are carrying him above the Conrail Viaduct and its canyon of railroad tracks. He may not even notice the rail lines below, because the two off-ramps for traffic frequently clog up with long lines of waiting cars, and he must be wary of impatient drivers impulsively veering into his path. This 400-foot-long stretch is completely encased in concrete to preserve the steel.

The Skyway proper begins above Tonnele Circle, the ground-level rotary that channels and directs traffic to the Holland and Lincoln tunnels and westbound Route 33—directs it, but slowly, like a cholesterol-clogged heart with an erratic beat. The black steel causeway carries the westbound driver across another line of Erie Railroad tracks, then climbs steeply to arch over the Hackensack River.

The mood of the drive, which has been tense since leaving the Holland Tunnel, now enters true white-knuckle territory. An access ramp, rising from Broadway in Jersey City at a steep 5.5 percent grade, debouches onto the Skyway, practically at the foot of the Hackensack River span. In defiance of every current traffic safety principle, the ramp opens into the left lane—the passing lane, the fast lane, with oncoming vehicles racing around a slight bend in the causeway. Meanwhile, the driver attempting to join the traffic must turn his head completely around to see oncoming vehicles.

The cars then hurtle up the Hackensack River span at an

angle that sometimes defeats older vehicles—stalled and overheated vans and cars are not uncommon on the Skyway. The
two narrow lanes of traffic in each direction are penned in by a
wall down the center of the causeway—an aluminum version
of the inverted-Y safety wall known across the country as the
Jersey barrier. There are no shoulders, just a three-foot-high
steel curb designed to keep careering vehicles from breaking
through the railings and tumbling down to the streets below.
Here, through the miracle of twentieth-century engineering,
it is possible to experience claustrophobia while driving over a
hundred feet in the air.

Police generally do not patrol the Pulaski Skyway—pulling
someone over for a ticket is tantamount to suicide in these
closely packed, high-velocity lanes—and drivers usually lead-
foot it through the entire three-mile stretch, whether to take
advantage of their freedom to speed or get the ordeal done
with as quickly as possible.

Cresting over the Hackensack River span, the driver glanc-
ing over his shoulder is treated to a vista of storage tanks, con-
tainer farms for tractor-trailers, and sparkling, dioxin-tainted
river water, all flickering like a Zoetrope image through the
steel I-beams lining the road. If the driver's eyesight is keen
and the air exceptionally clear, he will see the New Jersey
Turnpike's western spur rising from the marshes of Secaucus
and shouldering past the ancient rock pile known as Snake
Hill.

Now the driver descends as the causeway crosses the Meadowlands town of Kearny, and a new worry appears: an on-off
ramp for Kearny, opening off the left lane, causes a break in
the line of the Jersey barrier. When traffic is slow or jammed
up, drivers will sometimes use this gap to cross over to the other
side of the viaduct. This brings them into the oncoming fast

lane and a good chance of a fatal collision as oncoming cars roar down the blind curve.

The roadway rises again, not quite so steeply, for the second span over the Passaic River, then descends to rejoin U.S. Route 1-9 just north of Newark Liberty International Airport. During this descent there will be abrupt slowdowns for a right-lane turnoff onto Raymond Boulevard in Newark, and a final jolt of fear as the Skyway, curving sharply to the left, meets an eight-lane divided facility that sorts out Turnpike-bound traffic from vehicles headed for Route 22 and the Garden State Parkway. Inevitably, at least one driver in the left lane will realize he needs to be in the right lane, and in cutting over will set tires screeching and middle fingers jabbing a final time.

Few traffic facilities offer a driving experience as hairy as the Pulaski Skyway, and leaving it, many drivers probably wonder, "What idiot designed this thing?" or think, "Anybody could have done a better job than that."

And yet, the Skyway was not designed by idiots. The men who worked on the project were educated, adventurous, and eager to create a benchmark for all future traffic development. They were seasoned engineers who had worked on some of the greatest construction projects in history: the London Underground, the trans-Hudson railway tunnels, the Panama Canal, the Holland Tunnel, and the New York mass-transit system. At least one of them considered the project the capstone of his distinguished career, and his work earned him one of civil engineering's most prestigious awards.

They were visionaries who knew a great deal, but they applied what they knew in ways that turned out to be drastically inappropriate. We live with, and drive on, the consequences of those decisions.

•   •   •

Engineer Fred Lavis takes his ease in the countryside.
Undated photograph.

In the spring of 1924, a fifty-three-year-old consulting engineer named Fred Lavis found himself at loose ends. He had already designed and supervised the construction of railway lines in Central America, South America, and China, served as a consulting engineer on the immense Panama Canal construction project, and dabbled in village politics as a trustee in Scarsdale, New York. Along the way, Lavis had also found time to write four books about railroad location and design. With engineering assignments at a lull during the early 1920s, Lavis returned to Scarsdale and busied himself with local politics, photography, and lectures to engineering students at Yale, Princeton, and Rutgers universities.

"Swashbuckling" is not a word often associated with civil engineers, but Lavis's globetrotting career shows him to have been a restless man of great physical courage. An admiring profile written for an industry publication describes him as standing just over six feet, with steady blue eyes and an easy, booming laugh:

> Everything about the man connotes bigness—his hands, ears, bulbous nose, his hearty manner, and his great disdain for what might seem to be accepted opinion in most circles. "I'm a so-called rugged individualist," he described himself with an engaging, unboastful grin, and the expression in this case is no cliche, but an apt wordpicture.

Born on January 8, 1871, Lavis grew up in Torquay, a seacoast village in Devon on the channel coast of southwest England. At the age of sixteen, Fred Lavis sailed to America with his father, a merchant seaman named John Lavis, who had lost his savings on some bad investments and thought to make a fresh start with relatives in Boston. The elder Lavis quickly lost heart and returned to England, but his son remained in what he later called "the land of the bean and the cod." (A classic autodidact, Lavis appears to have had a weakness for curious turns of phrase.) Working as an errand boy for three dollars a week, supplemented by a two-dollar allowance from his relatives, young Lavis embarked on a self-improvement regimen, taking night classes in various subjects and hiring himself out as a tutor in algebra, a subject he had only just learned.

Lavis's entry to the railway industry came through a want ad in the *Boston Herald,* placed by a surveyor who required all applicants to send in an illustration of the Pythagorean theorem. Lavis submitted his diagram and was quickly hired to work as a "rod man" (the one who stands with the stadia rod, on which the "eye man" zeroes in through his instruments) for a little over twelve cents an hour. Once he had mastered that role, Lavis signed on with the Boston & Maine Railroad for a wharf-construction project along the Mystic River. By the time he was nineteen, Lavis was ready to join a survey crew bound for the southeast coast of Cuba, where a promoter hoped to locate an iron mine and build a railway and docks near Santiago de Cuba. The venture quickly collapsed, but not before Lavis received some training in the crucial job of transitman, who operates the tripod-mounted surveyor's transit. The instruction was delivered in the knockabout way that characterized most of Lavis's training:

> Shortly after we arrived, the transitman came down with fever and I was given his note book and told to run the instrument. I saw that he kept his notes running from the bottom to the top of the page, but did not know that that was the accepted practice. That night I went to the Chief Engineer and asked him why notes were kept this way instead of from top to bottom. He just looked at me, probably stumped himself, pointed his finger at me and yelled, "Get the hell out of here. Any goddamn fool ought to know that." So that was the way I was educated.

After the Cuban venture evaporated in 1892, Lavis sailed to Colombia for the first of many railway jobs that would bring him back again and again to South and Central America. Photos from the period show a trim young man with a thick mustache and a fondness for roughing it. He also seems to have been a bit of a ladies' man—many acquaintances attributed

his fluency in Spanish to the time-honored "sleeping diction-
ary" curriculum. Certainly by the time he was in Mexico to
work on the Chihuahua al Pacifico railroad, just before the
turn of the century, Lavis had acquired a young wife, about
whom he says remarkably little in his unpublished memoirs,
though the marriage ended with her death after about two
years. During their brief life together, Lavis brought her with
him to the railroad camps along the path of construction,
which had to be hacked and blasted through some of the
world's most spectacularly rugged territory, which ranged
from alpine conditions at the craggy Divisadero to nearly rain
forest humidity at the bottoms of innumerable deep canyons.
(In fact, the project, which had begun in 1880 with the grant-
ing of a government concession to utopian socialist Albert
Kinsey Owen, would not be completed until 1961 because of financial troubles and the difficulty of the work.)

In the parlance of the time, it was no place for a lady, as became clear when a wealthy young rancher invited Mrs. Lavis
to join him on a horseback ride through the countryside and
then tried to rape her. According to a newspaper account, a
friend took it upon himself to deliver "a severe thrashing" to
the assailant in Lavis's absence. A few days later, Lavis met his
wife's attacker in a railroad camp. Both men drew their pistols
and fired. Neither man was hit but Lavis's bullet felled the
other man's horse. Lavis left the Mexican pinned beneath the
dead animal and fled across the border to El Paso, thus avoid-
ing trouble with the law. Back in the States, Lavis took a
slightly less perilous job with the Choctaw, Oklahoma and Gulf
Railroad, locating rail lines through Indian territory that
would later be absorbed into the mighty fine Rock Island
Line.

Lavis paused just long enough to become a naturalized

American citizen and marry a second time. Over the next two decades, Lavis would crisscross the globe as a consulting engineer on projects in Central America (the Panama Canal), Argentina, Spain, Italy, and China before returning to America with the twenties in their full roar.

Back home in Scarsdale early in 1924 and already bored after a few months, Lavis took a train into the city for lunch at the Railroad Club of New York, where he ran into an old acquaintance, William G. Sloan. The New Jersey Highway Department had just gone through a spasm of scandals, and Hugh L. Scott, a retired general and former commander of Fort Dix, had been appointed to make a clean sweep. Sloan was Scott's choice for the post of state highway engineer.

Like Lavis, William G. Sloan was a railroad man to his last drop of heart's blood. He had served for several years as chief engineer for MacArthur Brothers, the great Chicago-based railroad company, but the dissolution of the company in the early 1920s confirmed that the automobile was supplanting the railroad engine. The lunch stretched out for two hours as the men discussed various projects on Sloan's desk, particularly a looming problem in Jersey City that demanded a speedy and radical solution.

Well before Clifford Holland staged his clandestine groundbreaking in 1922, state and local officials could see that the completion of the planned tunnel under the Hudson River would have a cataclysmic impact on Jersey City. The narrow, poorly laid-out streets were already virtually immobilized by local traffic and the omnipresent railway lines. During the year the tunnel project started, roughly 3.9 million vehicles crossed the Hudson River on the five ferries lining the Jersey City waterfront. Another 4.6 million vehicles crossed the

nearby Hackensack and Passaic river drawbridges. The opening of the tunnel would bring an estimated 18 million vehicles
into the heart of Jersey City. Without a new road to draw off
the traffic, the tunnel would become a long underground park-
ing lot, and the anticipated economic benefits of the new link
would evaporate in a cloud of automotive exhaust.

Sloan's job was to design a bypass that would channel the
traffic flood out of Hudson County and across the Meadowlands. New Jersey voters had already approved a forty-million-
dollar bond issue in 1922 to extend U.S. Route 1-9 from the city
of Elizabeth all the way to the portal of the tunnel, but after a
year of dithering the eight-member state highway commission had no plans drawn up. This prompted newly elected Governor George Silzer to dissolve the commission and replace it
with a slimmed-down four-man panel. The new commissioners were sworn in on March 13, and Sloan was appointed on
April 11, 1923.

The Holland Tunnel project was slated for completion in
1926. Sloan was immediately put in charge of an engineering
advisory board to estimate the amount of traffic that would
ride the thirteen-mile stretch between Elizabeth and Jersey
City, then suggest the best means for handling it. By early August, the advisory board's report was on Sloan's desk.

Throughout the fall and winter of 1923, Sloan and his staff
had considered the range of suggestions for the Route 1 Extension, including a proposal for a vehicular tunnel beneath the
prehistoric muck of the Meadowlands, from Newark all the
way to Bergen Hill. Sloan directed Lavis to pick his way
through the proposals and get the project moving. "He [Sloan]
said it was a problem for a railroad man," Lavis later wrote,
"especially one who, like myself, had been interested in the

economics of railroad location, of which few highway engineers had any conception."

Though he was leery of submitting himself to any large organization, let alone a government bureaucracy drenched in politics, Lavis could not resist the lure of a challenging design assignment. Lavis, who had returned from a railway project in Colombia only the year before, found himself working on the staff of the New Jersey Highway Commission.

According to Lavis, the fact that he was a New York resident was a barrier to his being hired by the state of New Jersey. Sloan's solution was to pay a visit to Frank Hague, whom Lavis called, in one of the occasional bizarre locutions that help give his memoirs their charm, "a politician of purest ray serene and 'the woiks' in New Jersey." (Perhaps Lavis was going for a play on vaudeville brogues.) Hague was putting all of his political clout behind the project: he'd gone to Trenton to explain to the legislature why the extension was significant for the entire state, not just Jersey City, and therefore had to be financed by the state. For all his dislike of politicians, Lavis ended up being impressed by Hague:

> I didn't like the idea of going to see a man like Hague but I couldn't see how it would do me any harm no matter what the result might be. I could still afford to be pretty independent. The situation was explained and all the comment Hague made was, "Bill, this is one of the biggest jobs ever started in Jersey and if you say this is the man to do it, get him busy." Pretty good for a dyed-in-the-wool politician but I have noticed that a lot of politicians have brains even if they have their own idea as to how they should be used. There was still some legal red

tape to unwind about the manner of making available the money for the work but finally in August of that year (1924), I established an office in Jersey City, got some men together and started surveys.

Lavis, like Sloan, was a disciple of Arthur M. Wellington and his book *The Economic Theory of the Location of Railways,* which had started in 1876 as a series of articles published in *Railroad Gazette.* The articles were gathered into book form the next year, and revised several times to produce a biblically proportioned tome (the sixth edition, issued in 1908, ran more than 970 densely printed pages) devoted to ruthlessly honing every detail of route location, grading, and curving in order to keep engineering and land-acquisition costs—as well as operating expenses for the rail companies—as low as possible.

Some of Wellington's dicta may seem laughably obvious now—it hardly needs noting that a steeply graded ramp will slow down vehicular traffic, resulting in time lost and gasoline burned. But America was only just beginning to learn about high-speed, high-volume mass transit, and only railroad engineering offered anything like guidance in designing new kinds of roads.

Ironically, Lavis's adherence to Wellingtonian principles had led him to question the Holland Tunnel design in the first place—he considered the project needlessly expensive and inefficient. So now it was his job to design a road capable of handling the traffic that would soon be pouring from the tunnel's mouth.

Lavis's partner on the project was another of Sloan's new hires: Sigvald Johannesson, a Danish-born engineer educated at the University of Copenhagen. Like the peripatetic Lavis, Johannesson had international experience: he had spent three years as an engineer with the London Underground, then moved to the United States in 1903 to work on the Hudson and Manhattan Railroad project—the series of railway tunnels beneath the Hudson River offering passenger service between Jersey City and Manhattan. Lavis had been a resident engineer on the project, so the two men were already familiar. Together, working under Sloan's direction, they would apply Wellington's lessons to the fledgling science of automotive highway design, and the creation of a new kind of road between Elizabeth and Jersey City.

The idea of designing highways along railroad principles may seem far-fetched now, but in the early decades of highway design it was a perfectly plausible way of doing things. Only two other methods had been used to transport large amounts of traffic across great distances—canals and railways—and of those only the railroads offered a land-based comparison.

Even before automobiles began clogging the nation's roads, railroad techniques were used for traffic control in cities. Since the nineteenth century, cities had coped with horse-drawn traffic by using hand-operated signs that resembled semaphore arms—at night, the signals were illuminated in the manner of railroad signals, with red meaning "stop" and green meaning "go."

Traffic control at intersections quickly became part of the standard roster of police duties, so it was probably inevitable that the first electric traffic light—a red-green signal controlled by hand—would be devised by a police officer: Lester Wire of Salt Lake City, Utah, who introduced it there in 1912. Unfortunately, Wire did not patent the device; that was done a year later by James Hoge, who added the words "stop" and "move" to the colored lenses. The new American Traffic Signal Company installed these throughout Cleveland, Ohio, in 1914.

By 1917, Lester Wire's initial traffic signal in Salt Lake City had grown into an impressive sequence of no fewer than six linked traffic signals, controlled by hand. Three years later, automatically controlled traffic lights were introduced in Houston, Texas. By then, traffic signal design had broken away from the railroad format by introducing an amber-colored warning light—this first appeared in New York and Detroit, and quickly spread throughout the country.

But the start-and-stop traffic flow created fresh problems: motorists do not react uniformly when the light flashes green, and slow-moving traffic turned into logjams on city streets. Within cities, it was just as well to have cars and trucks moving slowly, but outside populated areas it was preferable to keep things flowing smoothly, particularly in places where local roads intersected with higher-volume highways. Traffic circles, an English concept adapted for American use in 1915, grew less useful as traffic volumes increased. The challenge, then, was to create interchanges in which traffic control was encoded within the very design of the roads.

One of the earliest solutions was the "diamond" interchange, in which vehicles entering the highway from a local road were given direct access, but drivers leaving the highway would have to slow down and stop before joining local traffic. For intersections between high-volume roads, civil engineer Arthur Hale of Maryland came up with a two-level "cloverleaf" design that he patented in 1916. The first use of the design came in 1929, when a cloverleaf opened in Woodbridge, New Jersey, at what was then the intersection of Route 25 and Route 4 (now U.S. Route 1-9 and Route 35, just north of the present-day Woodbridge Center shopping mall), but the large amount of space needed to build a cloverleaf, combined with high real estate prices in urban areas, kept traffic planners from following the Woodbridge experiment for many years.

As more and more automobiles clogged the roads and the future outlines of modern-day commuter society began to take shape, civil engineers and traffic planners realized that something new was called for. The idealized form was described in 1918 by H. G. Shirley, Maryland's state highway commissioner, as a multilane thoroughfare with limited access, traffic flows separated by medians, shallow banked curves, and carefully graded hills with slopes of no more than 5 percent. Prototypes for the superhighway can be found as far back as the early 1900s, such as a twenty-mile circular road in Long Island (brainchild of car-racing enthusiast William K. Vanderbilt Jr.) that served as a racetrack and, during its off-hours, a connector road for some of the area's estates. But the first fully realized superhighway design in a densely populated urban setting would get a tryout on an uninviting patch of New Jersey marshland that had never seemed good for much of anything in the past, but would be the ideal setting for the roadway of the future.

For all his devotion to Wellington's principles, Lavis could see there would have to be some adjustments made. Rail lines were usually laid through undeveloped areas of the countryside, or the outskirts of cities, and therefore could be planned with very few conditions in mind other than economics. Highways, by contrast, were needed in areas that were already densely populated and developed, restricting the planner's design options and imposing additional restrictions, such as the cost for condemning and demolishing existing structures, and the need to keep clear of existing streets. Furthermore, Lavis noted in the 1927 article that laid out much of his thinking about highway design, rail lines were designed strictly for the profit of a single company. Major through-highways of the sort planned for the Route 1 Extension served a multitude of needs, many of them hard to quantify strictly in dollar terms, and would carry benefits far beyond the immediate neighborhood in which the highway was built.

The basic unit of Wellington's calculations was the train-mile, which took into account the cost of fuel, lubricating oil, track repairs, and car maintenance. The planner could then use train-miles to gauge the relative economic benefits of various railway locations.

Adapting Wellington's method, Lavis came up with the "car-minute," which he assigned a value of two cents. Lavis calculated that 3,600 vehicles would pass along the route each hour, making for 54,000 vehicles per day and 18,360,000 per year. To this, Lavis added the costs imposed by rising and falling road grades, tighter versus wider curves, the average expense of driving and maintaining automobiles, and the cost of time spent waiting at grade crossings or opened drawbridges. "It will be realized," Lavis wrote, "that a motor vehicle used for commercial purposes is just as much part of a manufacturing plant or selling organization as a machine in a factory, or an employee in a store. If idle when it might be working, it represents a unit of loss."

By calculating all of these elements, Lavis could then gauge how much each highway design would cost in terms of car-minutes, and how much money could reasonably be spent eliminating the problems. "I was convinced that the highway should be designed just as railways are designed," Lavis wrote, "to produce lowest ton-mile or passenger-mile costs, having due regard to original costs of construction, and costs of maintenance in relation to their effect on the operating costs of the vehicles. There was to be considered, also, the decreased costs of operation and of doing business on the streets of the by-passed cities."

But the considerations did not end there. The work of designing the Route 1 Extension—or Route 25, its confusing alternate designation—was also guided by what Lavis called "governing principles." In addition to funneling traffic to and from the Holland Tunnel, the road also needed to allow for a connection with the planned George Washington Bridge between Fort Lee and upper Manhattan. Various railroads had rights-of-way that they either would part with for sufficient money, or planned to keep for future development. The government of Jersey City—i.e., Frank Hague—wanted no more open cuts like the Erie Railroad train canyon, and the route through the city had to offer access to and from Hudson Boulevard, the main drag for much of Hudson County, and Tonnele Avenue. A ramp midway through the Meadowlands stretch was also required to promote development in the southern portion of Kearny.

There was also the question of how to get traffic across the Passaic and Hackensack rivers with minimal delays. The old Lincoln Highway route, which the Route 1 Extension was intended to supplant, already had two drawbridges so low to the water that they were constantly being opened for ship traffic, even pleasure craft, resulting in lengthy traffic backups. Resolving this question would bring politics into the mix and undermine most of the principles that Sloan, Lavis, and Johannesson brought to bear.

As they worked, planners and politicians became increasingly alarmed at the thought of what would happen if the

Route 1 Extension project became bogged down any further. Governor Silzer, speaking at a May 1924 conference on regional traffic problems, laid out the issues in plain language:

> We know that when the vehicular tunnel opens and the stream of cars that come from that tunnel are brought into the congested streets of Jersey City and Newark and the rest of the section, the tunnel will be absolutely worthless unless we make some provision to take care of those vehicles. . . . We cannot wait until the tunnel is opened and then start to solve the question.

The conference's follow-up report, issued in 1925, emphasized that the completion of a connection highway between Jersey City and Newark was "absolutely imperative," and its absence was "one of the most serious highway traffic problems in the New York region."

The path of the extension was divided into six sections for planning purposes, with the state advisory board suggesting alternate plans for three of the sections. As it turned out, the route Lavis and Johannesson designed—a diagonal route across the Meadowlands from Elizabeth to Bergen Hill—was nearly identical to the path suggested by the state advisory board. The stretch from Elizabeth to Newark would be built on an embankment with carefully graded curves, but for the swampy Meadowlands section the route became an elevated thoroughfare on concrete piers. The design dispensed with the suggested tunnel beneath the Meadowlands, which would have added another eight million dollars or so to the final project cost, and a different location for the highway cut through Bergen Hill. The advisory board's proposal had been uncomfortably close to the Erie Cut, and the railroad worried that any

plans it might make to expand the train canyon for more passenger lines would be hampered. As it turned out, additional
train traffic was not in the cards for the Erie Railroad—quite
the opposite, in fact—but as so often happened in the early
twentieth century, the wishes of the railroad company took
precedence.

The pressure to get moving on the Route 1 Extension project was such that work on the sections leading from the tunnel
mouth to the Bergen Hill cut began in the summer of 1925, before Lavis and Johannesson had finished their design work.
Over the next three years, sections of the superhighway were
completed and opened to use at either end of the project. But
the crucial middle was delayed by a lengthy series of squabbles
over what to do with the river crossings. Even after the Holland
Tunnel opened and traffic began rumbling up the ramp to the
Bergen Hill cut, the three-mile midsection of America's first
superhighway existed only on paper. Westbound drivers,
emerging from the Holland Tunnel, were channeled through
the depressed roadway and then forced to descend a ramp to
Tonnele Circle, where they joined the conga line of stalled vehicles waiting to get past the drawbridges across the Hackensack and Passaic rivers.

Since both rivers were navigable, they came under the juris-
diction of the federal War Department and the state Board of
Commerce and Navigation, both of which had a keen interest
in preventing any disruptions to the passage of barges and
tugboats. This was a great irritant to Lavis, who considered the
amount of actual ship traffic to be so negligible as to be
scarcely worth bothering about. At one point the War Department even demanded that the drawbridges along the old Lincoln Highway/Route 1 path be removed in exchange for
permitting the new spans. Since the diagonal highway was not

intended to provide access for local traffic, this demand would only create more problems for traffic control in the area. Lavis's solution was to submit a design calling for drawbridges at heights of thirty-five feet above each waterline for the final link in the Route 1 Extension. His thinking, he explained later, was that the height was sufficient to let the small amount of ship traffic pass beneath the spans. Larger ships could be routed through during times when traffic was at its lightest and opening the drawbridges would cause few problems.

Thinking his work complete, and heeding his wanderlust once again, Lavis resigned in 1928 to serve as a consulting engineer on railway projects in Guatemala and El Salvador. His designs for the Route 1 Extension earned him the 1930 Arthur M. Wellington Prize from the American Society of Civil Engineers. Sloan left his position in June 1929, leaving the project essentially an orphan when another round of infighting began.

The trouble actually began in January 1929, when the War Department—backed up by navigation interests along the rivers—flat-out refused to permit construction of any new bridges unless the Lincoln Highway spans were removed and replaced with a tunnel beneath the riverbeds. Sloan hurriedly appointed a three-member panel to study once again this most thoroughly studied of all traffic questions.

The compromise hammered out and approved in the fall of 1929 allowed the Lincoln Highway drawbridges to remain, but required the diagonal highway spans to be raised to 135 feet above the waterlines of the Hackensack and Passaic rivers— roughly four times higher than Sloan, Lavis, and Johannesson had envisioned. With every other section of the route already built and waiting to be linked, the ramps leading to the spans would have to rise at steep, engine-taxing grades, making a mockery of the Wellington-derived calculations Lavis had engineered into the design. To cut down on the amount of weight the higher spans would bear, Lavis's plans for concrete jacketing of the steel structures were also dispensed with, meaning there would be hefty tabs for maintenance down the road. There were plenty of other pitfalls awaiting motorists—pitfalls invisible to the men who had so relentlessly focused on car-miles and railway principles—but those would not be realized for another few years, after it was far too late to do anything about them.

Meanwhile, the pressure of traffic coming from the Holland Tunnel was unrelenting, and the need for relief increased almost by the day. Jacob L. Bauer, Sloan's successor as state bridge engineer, and engineer H. W. Hudson slammed through a new design, and the state highway department scrambled to get contracts awarded so the last three miles of the Meadowlands viaduct could be completed.

As the final phase of the Route 1 Extension began, all involved probably told themselves the worst of the fighting was behind them. As it turned out, the trouble had hardly even started.

CHAPTER 4

Rice Pudding

TEACHER: Who made the Jersey City Fire Department?

PUPIL: Mayor Hague.

TEACHER: Who made the Jersey City Police Department?

PUPIL: Mayor Hague.

TEACHER: Who made the world?

PUPIL: God made the world.

CHORUS OF PUPILS: You dirty Republican!

—*Hague-era joke popular in Jersey City*

The organization was a sacred word. The word "machine" was never used . . . that was an insult. A machine implied that there was some kind of a cold, automatic process that just ground out the votes. An organization implied that there was this hierarchy—from the top down—all these different levels of importance, different duties, different responsibilities. And most of them Irish. They were triumphing as a people after two centuries of humiliation in Ireland.

—Thomas Fleming, historian

During the 1890s, it was not uncommon for men swilling down nickel beers at the local tavern to line up a few Liberty

Heads in advance, so the suds would flow without interruption. It was also not unheard of for bartenders, swabbing down the bar amid the loud noises and distractions, to accidentally-on-purpose knock a few coins down into their palms as they buffed up the wood. This under-the-counter compensation was known as "rice pudding."

As the 1920s roared to their disastrous end, "rice pudding day" had become entrenched on the Jersey City calendar as the day municipal employees ponied up 3 percent of their annual salaries to Mayor Frank Hague's machine—or, as his minions preferred to call it, the organization. When Hague became mayor in 1917, the city payroll showed 1,745 employees; by 1928, that number had ballooned to 3,760. Since "rice pudding day" was handled on a strictly cash basis, the exact amount raised by the organization is a matter of conjecture. But except for the occasional grumbling of malcontents, who could be browbeaten into line or expelled from the payroll, the annual tithe was paid. After all, most employees were so well paid that even after serving up their share of pudding, they were still considerably ahead of their less-fortunate neighbors.

Combined with the take from fees paid by bootleggers, betting parlors, day-to-day bribery, and even legitimate operations, it added up to a formidable bankroll—enough to make the Hudson County organization the bulwark of Democratic strength in GOP-dominated New Jersey.

Hague and his people weren't the only ones with an angle. Many other ambitious, acquisitive players knew there was more than one way to get rice pudding. Sometimes getting it meant elbowing others out of the way. Sometimes the elbowing developed into a fight; sometimes the fight turned into something bigger.

Boiled down to its essentials, the power struggle that

erupted during the completion of America's first superhigh-way—the drawn-out series of battles that local newspapers called "the War of the Meadows"—was a fight over rice pud-ding.

During his thirty-year reign as one of America's top political bosses, Frank Hague was more than willing to explain his methodology to anyone who would listen. Newspaper colum-nist Joseph Alsop Jr., writing in 1936, described one such im-promptu lesson:

> He was talking in the dining room of one of the local ho-tels. He took the squares on the tablecloth to illustrate precincts and wards, tracing them out with his finger, as he explained the feudal system of American politics, whereby the precinct captain is governed by a ward lieu-tenant, the lieutenant by a ward leader, and each ward leader by the boss. "Suppose a good job comes along," he said. "Well, there's one ward that ought to get something; so I ask the leader to submit names. He gives me three names, and the third man on the leader's list is a good man, clean living, belongs to lodges, with a minor posi-tion, say $2,500 a year. Well, he's developed such effi-ciency that I think he's good. He's got the kind of leadership that we want to encourage. So I tell the ward leader, 'He's the man.' That's the way to keep your ma-chine going. Always deliver when a man delivers for you."

"Delivering" also applied to local residents. "When a person moves to Jersey City," journalist Dayton David McKean wrote, "his furniture van is often not unloaded before the block or dis-trict leader calls to see if there is anything he can do." Helping out included anything from calling to arrange water and mail service to introductions at the network of social and political clubs that allowed the Hague operation to manage and control political life. (In this, Hague benefited from Prohibition—before the Volstead Act, Jersey City's innumerable saloons functioned as independent political clubs.) The point was to ensure that whenever possible, the machine had a human face—a helpful, concerned one at that.

Historian Thomas Fleming grew up in Jersey City, and his father (along with several other relatives) was a Hague operative. That personal touch provided by canvassing, he recalled, was what distinguished the Hague operation from Tammany Hall, its elder sibling across the Hudson River:

> The people in Jersey City laughed at Tammany. They regarded them as sort of weary, worn out guys who didn't know how to do it anymore. They didn't canvass. My father used to say that in an appalled tone—"They don't *canvass!*" That was like saying a pilot didn't have a license or something to fly the plane. This was so basic in Jersey City: To get that vote out, you had to visit—that's all there was to it.

Under Hague, one observer recalled, there were "twelve ward leaders who learned, to their horror, that it was not enough to turn in as big a Democratic majority as last year's. It had to be bigger. I remember a situation in which the leader of a heavily Democratic ward apologized publicly to Hague because, in one of his districts, two Republican votes were counted. He promised that it wouldn't happen again."

Hague's practicality sometimes blurred into idealism. When women won the right to vote in 1920, Hague sponsored the political career of Mary Teresa Norton, who stood for election in the 1924 congressional race and served thirteen consecutive terms in the House of Representatives, where she helped guard the organization's flank in Washington, D.C., while also advancing the cause of women in government.

Hague's organization was not the only political machine in New Jersey, but his selectively moralistic stance contrasts favorably—until the mid-1930s, at any rate—with that of other political bosses. Hudson County's mirror image was the Republican-controlled Atlantic County political machine, which ran Atlantic City as a shoreside buffet for every popular vice. Under Republican boss Enoch "Nucky" Johnson, Atlantic City was considered a safe haven where gangsters could enjoy themselves without fear of reprisals from their competitors—so much so that in May 1929, crime bosses from across the country gathered for a national conference to work out the future of racketeering after Prohibition. Not only did Johnson host that conference—which drew Meyer Lansky, Dutch Schultz, and Al Capone, among others—but he was one of the kingpins in the Seven Group, which organized bootlegging activities up and down the eastern seaboard. Even allowing for the fact that gangsters were often considered folk heroes during the Prohibition era, that's a remarkable résumé for a public figure like Johnson.

For much of his reign, Hague faced criticism for permitting bootleggers and illicit gambling parlors to operate within Hudson County. Neither charge carries much weight decades later, when state governments vie for the privilege of letting casinos and lotteries bankrupt their citizens, and Prohibition is almost universally recognized as a harebrained social experiment that fostered contempt for the law and brought wealth and a measure of respectability to organized-crime figures.

Hague's tolerance of bootlegging and love of gambling gave

him some interesting acquaintances. Abner "Longy" Zwillman, New Jersey's representative at the 1929 gangster convention, was allowed to operate in western Hudson County and
Newark, under an arrangement in which Zwillman occasionally loaned out some of his "Minutemen"—Jewish boxing and
athletics enthusiasts, recruited at Newark gymnasiums—as
hired muscle to use against Hague's critics.

However, Hague's police force and its inner core of "zeppelins" did the bulk of the work to control and intimidate
Hague's opponents. One persistent critic, a burly pamphleteer
named Jefferson "Jeff" Burkitt, was beaten so regularly whenever he spoke on the street, it was hard to tell if the spectators
were there to listen or to witness the inevitable violence once
the cops arrived. After a particularly enthusiastic roughing up,
Burkitt confronted Hague during a city commission meeting
and asked to be allowed one public place to speak. Burkitt
spoke with one arm in a sling, one eye swollen and blackened.
Hague, studying the handiwork of his cops, started to laugh.
"Don't laugh at me, Mayor," Burkitt said. "I'm not laughing at
you," Hague replied, "but you look so goddamned funny."

Burkitt, like other Hague opponents, frequently found himself jailed on trumped-up charges. John Longo, another thorn
in Duh Mare's side, did a stretch for supposedly violating election laws—a richly ironic charge, considering the source. No
target was too small for the sledgehammer if it had succeeded
in irritating the boss. One local comedian who wrote humorous
letters to the editor about "City Haul" was charged with rape
after a prostitute entered his apartment, ripped her own
clothes, and screamed for help. The county jail was in Secaucus, in a fetid patch of swamp near Snake Hill, the ancient pile
of traprock that rises incongruously from the southeastern portion of the Meadowlands. At one time a leprosy hospital and an

insane asylum, the county jug was so foul that Hudson County operatives nicknamed it "Devil's Island" and assigned men to work there as a punishment detail. During heavy rains, swamp water tainted with industrial effluent and offal from the area's many hog farms would flood the building and swirl across the cell floors. Doing a stretch at Devil's Island was enough to silence most naysayers, if it didn't send them out of the state entirely.

During his day, Hague was often painted as the maestro of voting fraud, and there can be little doubt that many of the ward-heeler tricks he learned during his days as street muscle for the Democratic Party were resurrected with a few refinements. One common maneuver, which long predated the Hague era, was to postpone the state-mandated updates of voting rolls for several years at a time. Sometimes people who had moved out of Jersey City years earlier learned they had cast ballots in the city's most recent elections; sometimes people who had died subsequent to the previous update showed their commitment to democracy by continuing to vote. Thus was born the legend of Hague the man who could make the dead come to life on election day. This would be cemented in the late 1930s by a classic *New York Post* cartoon depicting Hague as the angel Gabriel, using his horn to summon ghosts who stand in line to cast ballots alongside household pets, children, and asylum inmates accompanied by their guards.

But the majority of Hague's election victories were won through matchless organizational skills, close attention to detail, and an unrivaled gift for strategy, honed through a series of duels with the New Jersey state legislature, which was dominated by Republicans well greased with cash from railroad interests.

Though Jersey City had a four-mile waterfront, only about 140 feet of it was accessible to city residents—the rest was held by the railroads. Elsewhere in the state, railroads paid municipal taxes of $18,000 per acre on the land they used; in Jersey City, they paid only $3,000. Once he became mayor, Hague set out to change things in typical blunderbuss fashion. Standard Oil saw its tax levy jump from $1.5 million to $14 million, while the Public Service Company utility was presented with a tax bill for $30 million, well up from the previous $3 million. The combined tax bill for the railroads soared from $67 million to $160 million. The state Board of Taxes and Assessments promptly voided the increases. Hague saw that control of a single county in a GOP-ruled state was obviously not going to be enough.

For most of Hague's reign, New Jersey was a largely agricultural state with only two cities big enough to be worthy of the name: Jersey City and Newark. Hudson County's massed voting bloc ensured that no Democrat could expect to win the party's nomination in a gubernatorial race without Hague's backing. Furthermore, that bloc could then be used to give the Democratic candidate a guaranteed edge in the polls come November. Hague's first hand-picked candidate was a Jersey City banker named Edward I. Edwards, who served as governor from 1920 to 1923. Two more Hague men had their turns in the governor's seat: George Sebastian Silzer and A. Harry Moore. This gave Hague the power to vet appointments to the New Jersey judiciary, which at the time was a patchwork of duchies like the Court of Errors and Appeals (the state's highest court under the 1844 vintage constitution) and the Orphans' Court. These served as a bulwark against legal attacks on the organization and made Hague's operatives virtually immune from prosecution.

Since the state constitution barred a governor from serving successive terms, Moore would not be able to run in 1928. This was a problem, since the leading Republican gubernatorial hopeful, Robert Carey, was one of Hague's most dedicated enemies. There was also a presidential race between Republican Herbert Hoover and Democrat Al Smith, Hague's close friend, and the threat of a Republican sweep was in the offing.

By the time the votes were counted in the May 15 primary, it became clear that Hague had pulled off something rather brilliant: he'd arranged for some 20,000 Hudson County Democrats to vote as Republicans. These "One-Day Republicans" threw the GOP nomination to a Perth Amboy engineer named Morgan F. Larson, whom Hague considered more tractable than Carey. The uproar only grew louder when it turned out that 1,300 of those Republicans were from the Horseshoe. "Who knew there were 1,300 Republicans in the Horseshoe?" crowed the *Jersey Journal*, which offered a reward to anyone who could find them.

As it turned out, Larson was a lot less tractable than Hague had figured, and the scandal over the One-Day Republicans resulted in an investigation by the state senate. The hearings were legislative opera buffa, chronicled with obvious relish by the region's newspapers, with committee members presiding like WASP straight men over a procession of clownish Hague appointees who might have been taken straight from a vaudeville stage, or a particularly vicious Thomas Nast cartoon.

There was veterinarian J. L. Lindsay, paid three thousand dollars a year to attend to the aches and pains of the cow population of Hudson County, which at the time numbered about seventy-five animals. (Asked if the job was unduly taxing, Lindsay replied: "No, they were pretty healthy. They don't require much attention.") There was Sheriff John J. Coppinger,

who could not name most of his staff and could offer no justifi-
cation for his eleven-thousand-dollar annual salary aside from
the fact that he signed plenty of checks. And, above all, there
was Albert H. Mansfield, the bulky health and sanitary inspec-
tor for Hudson County, whose real duties seemed to be wearing
a white apron and presiding over a speakeasy called the Semi-
nole Club. Asked why he could not produce the membership
records for the club, Mansfield—imperturbable and unreach-
able behind an immense walrus mustache and a blandly inex-
pressive face—opined that they must have been stolen by
Republicans trying to do him in.

The two main players, state senator Clarence Case and New
Brunswick attorney Russell Watson, were comfortable with
the circus atmosphere: both had been part of the defense team
for accused killer Frances Hall during the gaudy Hall-Mills
murder trial of 1926. (Since Hague had been one of the figures
urging that the case be reopened after the initial investigation
bogged down, both Case and Watson had a personal as well as a
political score to settle.) Case's trademark mannerism was to
lower his face and peer over his granny spectacles in feigned as-
tonishment at what he was hearing, and he had plenty of
chances to use it when Frank Hague entered the assembly
chamber to a mingled chorus of cheers, boos, and catcalls.
Hague, dapper and smiling, flat-out refused to answer most of
the questions about how a man whose salary never rose above
eight thousand dollars a year could afford a mansion in the exclusive Jersey Shore community of Deal, a luxurious duplex
apartment on Duncan Avenue in Jersey City, and another get-
away home in Florida. What means did the mayor of Jersey
City use to accumulate such wealth? "Only my brain and my
ability to see things," was the closest Hague came to a mean-
ingful reply. When the committee found Hague in contempt

for his stonewalling, the Court of Errors and Appeals ruled that the committee had overstepped its bounds. More than a decade would pass before the GOP took another run at Hague's organization.

But the Case Commission did score one solid blow against Hague. The testimony of so many witnesses about Duh Mare's lavish lifestyle drew the interest of the U.S. Treasury Department, which decided in 1929 to review Hague's income tax records. These were found wanting, and after about a year of negotiations, Hague agreed to pay a sixty-thousand-dollar penalty.

What happened next puzzled many observers. Hague was obviously a wealthy man. And yet he did not pay the penalty—it was paid for him by an associate, a labor leader named Theodore M. Brandle, or "Teddy."

Even as bridge designers were taking advantage of innovations in steelmaking technology and building techniques to create a network of dazzling spans across America, architects were learning how to build office towers that matched the empire-building dreams of their tenants: bigger, more ambitious, and, most important, higher. By using frameworks of steel, rather than thick walls of masonry, to support a building's weight, architects could come up with ever more gravity-defying designs. Chicago's Home Insurance Building, built in 1885, may seem like a comic place to begin—at only ten stories high, it would barely qualify as a mid-rise by today's standards—but its underlying steel frame construction made it the undeniable ancestor of this new breed of building, which did not use its own masonry foundation and walls to stay upright. Buildings increasingly became steel skeletons upon which the facade was hung, a design that permitted greater and greater heights of construction. And as the buildings grew loftier, they were given a name once used for the light sail flapping at the top of a ship's mast—skyscraper.

At first, the ironworkers who welded together the steel skeletons were considered the lowest on the pecking order of craftsmen involved in constructing an office building—compared with carpenters, who kept their wages high by enforcing a lengthy period of demanding apprenticeship, ironworkers were seen as a bunch of burly goons whose value lay in the brute strength they used to manhandle steel beams and girders into place.

But as the skyscrapers rose ever higher and the work of erecting them became ever more dangerous, ironworkers began to see themselves as a breed apart—unique in their appetite for risk and aptitude for violence. "Only men of great physical strength and courage became skyscraper men," wrote labor historian Louis Adamic. "Putting their lives in daily danger as they did, they developed a psychology of recklessness and violence that people in less hazardous occupations may find difficulty in understanding."

Under these circumstances, it seems entirely predictable that union leaders from the early years of the ironworkers' history would be brawlers like Sam Parks, a semiliterate bully who wielded complete control over New York construction sites from 1896 to 1903. Parks was one of the original union "walking delegates," not connected to any one employer or job but expected to range across several job sites each day, able to negotiate with employers on the spot and call strikes at the drop of a rivet. Since the job often involved going toe-to-toe with an employer's hired thugs, exceptional toughness was required.

The construction industry is uniquely vulnerable to outside

pressure. Many different types of craftsmen are involved in the construction of a large building, and their work must be choreographed with almost balletic precision. The builder has taken out large loans at high interest rates; quite often he has equity partners demanding a quick return on their investment. A delay in one area of the construction project translates into additional expense, and a longer wait before the building is finished and ready to generate income through rent-paying tenants.

This makes builders a little more willing, perhaps, to buy off trouble. It certainly made Sam Parks and his colleagues a little more willing to accept payment for making labor trouble go away. Though Parks's salary as a walking delegate was fairly meager, he had a lot of money in the bank, lived well, and kept his wife in diamond jewelry. This aroma of criminality, combined with an autocratic style and penchant for violence, earned men like Sam Parks the unofficial title "labor czars," and in time they would come to represent as much of a threat to labor as determined enemies like the National Erectors' Association.

This overheated, combative environment produced Teddy Brandle, a Jersey City native, born in 1884, who came of age during the high noon of the labor czar era but offered a smoother, less thuggish version of the Parks style. Like Hague, Brandle appears to have been something of a late bloomer in the arena of politics: not until Brandle reached his forties was there any sign that he had any ambitions beyond those of a union delegate. Brandle had the sturdy build of most iron-workers, augmented by matinee idol looks and Rotarian gregariousness. These qualities and his energetic support work during a number of strikes led to Brandle's winning appointment as the business agent for the Ironworkers Local 45 in Jer-

sey City. He quickly gained control of several other construction union locals throughout northern New Jersey and topped
it off by heading a business association for the construction industry.

In hindsight, it is difficult to see the qualities that earned
Brandle praise even from those who later considered him an
enemy and a blot on the image of labor. In his book *The Lean
Years*, labor historian Irving Bernstein speaks of "the amazing
Teddy Brandle—businessman, banker, politician, employer-
association mogul." Another critic of the era, Harold Seidman
of *The Nation*, called Brandle "no ordinary man," even as he
condemned Brandle as a second-generation labor czar and
crook. The burst of energy that ultimately turned Brandle into
a one-man business conglomerate, half gangster and half entrepreneur, would be unlocked through his alliance with Frank
Hague.

It's hard to say when Hague and Teddy Brandle first became
acquainted. In all likelihood, the two met while Hague was
commissioner of public safety. During the years 1915 and
1916, Hague went out of his way to court the support of the
New Jersey State Federation of Labor, and two of its con-
stituent unions in particular: the Hudson County Building
Trades Council and the Hudson Central Labor Union. At a
time when government officials were usually on the side of
employers in any labor dispute, Hague stood out as a man who
would actually send the police to turn back strikebreakers. Before giving him too much credit for this, it should be noted that
Hague had crushed the nascent policemen's union during his
term as commissioner of public safety, and that the bulk of Jersey City's industrial base used unskilled and semiskilled workers of no interest to the American Federation of Labor. By

cultivating the building trades, Hague was ingratiating himself with the chief paladins of union activity in Hudson County.

According to *New York Post* reporter Leo Katcher, Hague and Brandle had a mutual acquaintance in Arnold "the Big Bankroll" Rothstein, the racketeer reputed to have fixed the 1919 World Series. Katcher, whose 1959 biography of Rothstein is long on hearsay but short on footnotes and citations—not surprising, considering his subject's cautious habits and Katcher's reliance on sources like mobster "Lucky" Luciano—claimed that Rothstein helped out in 1917 by deputizing Tammany Hall floaters to cross the Hudson and vote for Hague. Rothstein's reward was a bookmaking franchise in Hudson County, which eventually became so famous for illegal off-track betting that newspaper columnist Westbrook Pegler dubbed it "the Horse Bourse."

Brandle's chief source of rice pudding was his card-index system, which he used to keep track of which union members were in his favor and which needed to be taught a lesson—or blackballed entirely. Those who worked kicked back a portion of their pay.

Brandle proved his worth to Hague in the 1924 presidential race, when Progressive Party candidate Robert M. La Follette espoused a platform calling for, among other things, a shift of the tax burden to the high-income brackets and government ownership of the nation's railroads and power-generating resources, which the party saw as being mismanaged by private interests. The national leadership of the American Federation of Labor had abandoned its long-held position of neutrality to endorse La Follette, and many of New Jersey's unions were inclined to support the Wisconsin progressive. Hague, as a loyal Democrat, supported party nominee John W. Davis, and he enlisted Brandle to head off any endorsements for La Follette from the New Jersey building trades unions. Brandle persuaded the unions to stay out of the race. The effort may have been unnecessary—both Davis and La Follette were buried in the landslide that swept Calvin Coolidge into the White House—but Hague was grateful for Brandle's help.

The connection with Hague opened doors for Brandle, and he was quick to exploit them. Brandle hooked up with Joseph Hurley, a state assemblyman based in Hudson County, and together they launched Branleygran, a firm that underwrote the completion bonds required for all big construction projects to ensure that if the developer went bankrupt, there would still be money on hand to finish the job. The bonding company on a big project reaped lucrative fees, and the link with Hague (and through him, the governor's office) ensured that a significant percentage of state construction projects would require bonds from Branleygran.

This proved especially profitable when Hague embarked on what will probably be his most enduring legacy to Jersey City: the creation of a downtown business area. Jersey City, stitched together from a number of separate towns and then cut into pieces by railway lines, had never enjoyed a traditional central business district. Hague's vision, which he set to work realizing in the mid-1920s, involved demolishing several blocks at the area where Hudson Boulevard crossed over the deep cut for the Pennsylvania Railroad and the station for one of the Hudson Tubes. The mayor envisioned it as a nucleus for Jersey City's further development, and a showcase for motorists coming up from the Holland Tunnel. A wide traffic bridge across the railroad cut helped unify the district. Branleygran, the construction unions, and even the construction companies Brandle owned on the side all benefited from the creation of Journal

Square, which was to become the setting for the jewel in Brandle's crown.

In 1923, the American Federation of Labor began urging its members to fight capital with capital by forming banks owned and controlled by unions, which would pool the fees and dues paid by their members in order to increase their economic muscle. The locals were quick to respond, particularly in New Jersey. A year after the AFL urged its members to think big, several Paterson-based locals representing workers in the city's silk-weaving plants formed the Labor Cooperative Bank. A year later, Newark saw the opening of the Union National Bank.

Never a man to miss a trick, Brandle launched the Labor National Bank in June 1926. The nominal founder of the institution was the Union Labor Investment Corporation, of which Brandle was the majority shareholder.

One of the last survivors of the era was Esther Meers, a Jersey City woman who worked as a secretary in Brandle's office. (Actually, her duties included bookkeeping and insurance-policy underwriting, but the social mores of the time dictated that she would be classified and paid only as a secretary.) At age ninety-three, her most vivid memories were of the times that Brandle brought one of his associates or labor subjects into his office for a dressing-down. "He had quite a way with the English language," Meers said. "I was just glad he didn't use it on me."

At first the bank operated from the ground floor of the Universal Building, one of the new structures going up around Journal Square. But with the dues from forty-one north Jersey locals pouring into the bank's coffers, Brandle wanted a structure commensurate with his ambitions and new standing.

Almost a year to the day after the Labor National Bank was

founded, its new headquarters started to rise on four vacant lots
where Sip Avenue joined with Journal Square, next door to the
spiffy new headquarters of the *Jersey Journal*. At the time of
its completion, a year later, the fifteen-story neoclassical con-
fection was the tallest building in Jersey City (it is still the
tallest in Journal Square). On the first day of August 1928,
Frank Hague and Governor A. Harry Moore led a straw-hatted
swarm of politicians and labor leaders out of the swampy summer heat and into the deep, cool shade of the new building's
long lobby, past a bank of elevators and marble-lined walls,
into the marble- and wood-trimmed bank itself, where tellers
awaited customers under a barrel ceiling of green, yellow, and
blue stained glass. The center of Teddy Brandle's empire was
open for business.

Brandle's vision of "serving all sides" had been realized.
Across northern New Jersey, anybody who wanted to cement
bricks or weld steel into a building had to reckon with the czar.
He had, as he once promised, built a fence around the northern
half of New Jersey and made it his kingdom. At the governor's
direction, bond fees from construction projects all over the
state—including projects growing out of the new, improved
Journal Square—were pouring into his Branleygran firm. If
he called a strike, Brandle knew the mayor would send Jersey
City's legendarily rough police to halt any strikebreaking.

This was the high noon of Brandle's power, and he owed
most of it to the goodwill of Frank Hague, whose philosophy
of government was simple: "Play ball with me and I'll make
you rich."

How did the relationship between Hague and Brandle go sour?
Appropriately enough for a conflict involving construction
work, the flash point for the War of the Meadows was a build-

ing. A complex of buildings, to be more precise: the Jersey City Medical Center, which during the course of Hague's administration would grow into a sprawling art deco complex that dominated the skyline along Bergen Hill and served as the crown jewel of his thirty-year reign.

The center reflected Hague's obsession with health—growing up in the pesthole of the Horseshoe had made him a lifelong hypochondriac—but it also reflected good politics. By the time of its completion in 1941, the center was the third largest medical facility in the world, with 1,800 beds and a top-notch staff whose services were rendered effectively free of charge. "Have your baby or your operation on the mayor" was an oft-heard boast during the Hague era, making loyalty to the organization literally a cradle-to-grave affair. Every Christmas, the medical center's Christmas tree and Nativity scene drew swarms of visitors, and children unfortunate enough to be in the hospital would get a personal visit from Santa Claus, escorted by Hague. In Hudson County, even jolly old Saint Nick put out for the Boss.

The first building in the complex was the Margaret Hague Maternity Hospital, named after the mayor's mother, who had delivered him and other babies on the kitchen table. If any building could certify the rise of the Irish Americans of Hudson County to a pinnacle of success, it was this building—designed to end a century of fetid conditions that had given the Horseshoe a heartbreaking infant mortality rate. No expense was spared in its construction, and Hague saw to it that the staff was equipped with top-of-the-line Cadillac ambulances. As more buildings rose, Hague began to spend as much time at the medical center as he did at City Hall, slipping in and out of a mahogany-paneled office with a secret back door. He was known for prowling the medical center's halls, ready to pounce

on any cigarette stubs or bits of litter. Hague would even travel
to different parts of the city and call in false alarms, simply to
gauge the response time of the ambulance crews, and woe be-
tide the intern who appeared to be dragging his feet. At best,
he could expect a good bawling out; at worst, a punch in the
mouth from the enraged mayor. The Jersey City Medical Center was Frank Hague's obsession. Only the most reckless kind
of fool would interfere with it. As it turned out, such a fool was
close at hand.

In the fall of 1931, a Newark contractor named Leo Brennan
was hired to build a powerhouse to ensure the continued
smooth operations of the Jersey City Medical Center even during a power failure. Brennan was happy to play by the rules,
but only so far. He hired union men for his work crew, but he
refused to work through Teddy Brandle's card-file system.
Since Brennan's contract had already been approved without first going through Brandle, the labor czar was doubly
annoyed.

Brandle's first step was to call a strike on the job site,
but Brennan's men—like Brennan himself—would not stop.
Brandle then sent some bullyboys to roust the workmen; after a
brawl in which several of Brennan's men were badly beaten,
the Jersey City police stepped in and shut down the site. Brennan surprised all observers when he marched off to court and
won an order allowing the work to continue.

Brandle went to Hague and threatened a strike that would
shut down all work on the medical center. Hague took the un-
usual step of brokering a deal with Brennan. Though the powerhouse job had barely been started, Brennan received full
payment for the job, and another firm was appointed through
Brandle's list of approved contractors. Having to pay twice for

the same work generated a cost overrun, and Hague was forced to go before the Hudson County governing board, homburg in hand, to ask for the extra money.

There was never any doubt that the freeholders would approve the funding, but Hague found the entire conflict personally embarrassing, and he was not a man to forget such a thing. Reporters began hearing rumors of the mayor and the union boss engaging in loud, violent arguments at City Hall. Brandle, using that command of the English language noted by Esther Meers, apparently gave as good as he got; moreover, the strapping labor czar was not someone Hague could intimidate physically.

Brandle was indeed a powerful man, but he appears to have forgotten that the very cornerstone of his empire was his relationship with Hague. He also appears to have forgotten, or missed, one of Machiavelli's sternest maxims: If you strike at a prince, you must kill him. Brandle had struck at the ruler of Hudson County, the man with a direct pipeline to the halls of state power, and succeeded only in angering him.

Hague, for his part, knew there was more than one way to best an opponent, and if the direct approach failed, there were plenty of roundabout ways to reach the same goal. Even as the medical center dispute reached its climax, Brandle was already locked in combat with a much bigger, even more ruthless antagonist than Hague. All he had to do was take a wrong step, and Hague would have him where he wanted him.

CHAPTER 5

Burned Bridges

If a man says to me the McNamaras should be condemned, my reply is: All right, we will condemn the McNamaras; but we will also condemn the Carnegies and the Steel Trust. If a man says to me that the Iron Workers' Union should be condemned, I say: All right, but we will also condemn the National Erectors' Association. Before the union began to use dynamite, their men lived on starvation wages, some of them on less than $400 a year, with families! If they say, we want light on the activities of union men, I say: All right, but light up the Steel Trust also. Light up both labor and capital. Put on the searchlights and we are willing that our sins should be compared with the sins of the employers.

—Anton Johannsen, labor organizer, 1913

The apple peddler, that emblematic figure from the early years of the Depression, did not appear on city streets until the fall of 1930. By that time, the public had heard a year's worth of predictions about renewed prosperity being just around the corner. But during October of 1929, a pair of stock-market crashes caused billions of dollars in value to evaporate. By March 1930—a month before work on the high-level viaduct over the Meadowlands got under way—millions of jobs had followed suit. By 1933, the year the recently completed viaduct was named the Pulaski Skyway, there would be 14.5 million unemployed.

But for ironworkers, times were pretty good. Privately funded construction projects begun during the flush years of the 1920s, such as the Empire State Building, continued into the 1930s. Just as they were petering out, publicly funded projects of immense scale and ambition stepped into the gap: the Golden Gate Bridge in San Francisco; the McCullough Memorial Bridge over Coos Bay and the Lewis and Clark Bridge across the Columbia River, both in Oregon; the San Francisco-Oakland Bay Bridge. Robert Moses, with the unassuming title of parks commissioner for New York, made himself into the patron saint of ironworkers with the Triborough Bridge, a sprawling complex of bridges and viaducts linking Manhattan with the Bronx and Queens—a construction project so big that its demand for materials rekindled furnaces in some fifty Pennsylvania steel mills and drew on the full-out production capacity of cement plants as far west as the Mississippi River.

The long, spasmodic struggle between labor and employer that began after the Civil War is a perfect illustration of Nietzsche's warning about the danger of becoming the image of what one fights against.

With the rapid industrialization of the late nineteenth century came the decline of craft-based production. Factories produced goods better, cheaper, and above all faster than the old methods, and in this new scheme of things the employee was another replaceable part. Immense fortunes were created as new industries rose across the country, and under the distorted, sinister version of evolutionary theory called "social Darwinism," the men who commanded the top of the heap were God's chosen aristocrats, and those who labored for them could either seek work elsewhere or stay and submit to the control of their betters.

If Andrew Carnegie and Henry Clay Frick wanted their steelworkers at Homestead, Pennsylvania, to live in company housing, pay inflated prices for company-supplied groceries with company scrip, and rent houses at above-market rates, then who dared to argue with them? If George Pullman's employees were willing to build railroad cars according to his dictates, why should they balk at living in Pullman, Illinois, and having their lives managed according to his dictates? If the market slowed down and sales dropped, who were the employees to complain if wage cuts followed? And if they decided to make an issue of it anyway, there were always fresh waves of immigrants stepping off boats ready to work.

Sooner or later, however, those immigrants started asking themselves the same questions that had plagued their predecessors. If Andrew Carnegie could buy himself a castle in the Scottish Highlands, why couldn't he manage a slightly higher hourly wage for the men whose dangerous labor helped pay for the castle? Was it so unreasonable that a man should demand to be viewed as something more than a source of profit for other men? Why should laborers risk their bodies in the steel mills and coal mines and expect nothing but a curt farewell when their health finally gave way? With these questions came successive labor organizations—the Knights of Labor, quickly followed by the Industrial Workers of the World—and in each case the response of the employers was to go to war.

This was the period in which a Swedish immigrant laborer named Joel Hägglund, better known today as Joe Hill, was convicted of murdering a Salt Lake City man and his son on evidence that said little about Hill's guilt but volumes about his status as a union organizer for the IWW. This was when "Big Bill" Haywood, leader of the Western Federation of Miners and a cofounder of the IWW, was the target of numerous prosecution attempts that finally hit pay dirt when he was convicted of espionage in 1918. This was when textile workers in Lawrence, Massachusetts—most of them women and girls barely into their teens—went out on strike and found themselves surrounded by guardsmen with fixed bayonets, judges ready to send them to jail for throwing ice at the textile mill windows, and police ready to club down women as they gathered at the local train station to send their children to stay with supporters during the strike—all so mill owners could impose wage cuts on employees who were already living on molasses and beans. This was when a 1914 strike by coal miners in Ludlow, Colorado, turned into a massacre as state militiamen attacked the tent city where strikers and their families had taken shelter.

It was a war in which labor was forever overmatched by the employers' ability to dictate the terms of battle, change the nature of the battlefield, and influence the way each battle was covered in the national press. It was a war in which the blame for outbursts of violence usually fell on workers and union organizers, whose moral capital was forever in danger of being lost through a single misstep or strategic error. Meanwhile, employers used spies to disrupt union meetings and foment extremism, and employed detective agencies—essentially hired thugs—to threaten and beat down union organizations. One of the most fearsome was the semilegendary Pinkerton agency, which had established itself as the most ruthless and brutal strikebreaking operation in America. One of its operatives was a young man named Dashiell Hammett, who after three years of watching the agency at work (and participating in some of its strikebreaking) quit to become a writer. His first novel, *Red Harvest*, was published in 1929, almost the verge of the Skyway labor war, and the story remains notable for its matter-of-fact depiction of a coal-mining town where the police, the city, and the local gangsters have banded together to destroy all attempts at union organization.

It was a war in which employers could, if all the other means at their disposal failed, rely on the local, state, and federal governments to send reinforcements to keep employees in their place. When fights erupted between union workers and the nonunion "scabs" hired to dispossess them, newspapers might wring their hands over the violence, but they seldom pointed their fingers at the men who set the two sides fighting. And the labor movement that had started with the idealism of the nonviolent Knights of Labor had, by the 1920s, been transformed into something almost as violent as its opponents.

In no other industry was this warfare as relentlessly vicious as the steel industry.

Teddy Brandle's nemesis, and the agent of Frank Hague's revenge, was the National Erectors' Association, an organization forged in 1907 during the wild clashes of the roughneck Sam Parks era of labor czars. The American Bridge Company was its organizer and guiding light, but the organization's membership roster bristled with formidable names: the McClintic-Marshall Company, Post & McCord, the Phoenix Bridge Company. These firms were sworn to what they called the "American Plan." The underpinnings of the philosophy, when cleared of cant about "open shops" that were open to all comers, were purely economic: they wanted employees who would work as cheaply as possible.

In his book *Dynamite,* a study of class warfare in the United States, the writer Louis Adamic called the National Erectors' Association "one of the most determined and brutal open-shop employers' organizations in the United States. . . . [A]bout forty of the largest erecting concerns in the country belonged to the Association, a number of them subsidiary companies of the fanatically anti-union Steel Trust, and they waged, individually and collectively, a relentless war against the Iron Workers, who, as the lowest paid of the building trades, were trying hardest to improve their lot." The NEA was an organization of manufacturers who pooled their efforts in order to keep employees from pooling their efforts. It called union officials like Teddy Brandle criminals, then hired criminals to fight them. The NEA's drive to break the back of the International Association of Bridge and Structural Ironworkers was so ruthlessly effective that a small cabal of union men responded by embarking on the "Dynamite Conspiracy" of 1907–11, crisscrossing the country by rail to sabotage nonunion construction projects. The plot culminated on October 1, 1910, with the detonation of the *Los Angeles Times* building, the headquarters of the rabidly antiunion publisher Harrison Gray Otis. The explosion killed twenty-one people and touched off a nationwide manhunt that ended with the arrest of John McNamara, the secretary-treasurer of the ironworkers union, as well as his older brother James McNamara and fifty-four union members. John was accused of masterminding the cross-country plot, and at first his case aroused national interest and sympathy. Then, on December 1, 1911, James pleaded guilty to the *Times* bombing, while John pleaded guilty to a lesser charge. The backlash effectively killed the union movement in Los Angeles and nearly wrecked the career of famed defense attorney Clarence Darrow, who had agreed to represent the brothers against his better judgment.

All of this bloody history loomed in the background as the state highway department rushed to complete the Route 1 Extension project. During the dithering and negotiations with the War Department over the two river bridges, the bulk of the project had been completed. The long stretch from Elizabeth to Newark had been graded, prepared, and paved as a gleaming white causeway ready to funnel armies of cars and trucks through the most densely populated section of New Jersey. The design (very little of which survives south of the Skyway today) took northbound drivers past the gritty waterfront and the factories of Elizabeth, and across the swampy edge of Newark and the reeking clouds from its tanneries, past the fledgling Newark Airport to the very threshold of the Meadowlands. And there it stopped.

The four contractors chosen to complete the last three miles of the Route 1 Extension were all mainstays of the National Erectors' Association. The American Bridge Company was given the contract for the easternmost portion of the viaduct, from the section above Tonnele Circle to the threshold of the Hackensack River bridge. McClintic-Marshall was chosen for the core of the project: the two cantilever bridges across the Hackensack and Passaic rivers. Phoenix Bridge was given the job of building the connection between the two bridges, while the Taylor Fichter Company was assigned work on either end of the Meadowlands section. Work was set to begin in April 1930.

Brief descriptions of the Skyway labor war are found in newspaper articles about Hague, as well as the two key books about Hague's reign: *The Boss* by Dayton David McKean and *A Cycle of Power* by Richard Connors. While both assume that Hague insisted on making the Meadowlands project an open-shop job, simply as a blow against Brandle, there is no reason to think that Hague could have influenced any of the contractors on this issue. These four companies were battle-hardened, well-blooded veterans of labor clashes across the country, and their membership in the National Erectors' Association certified them as implacable opponents of organized labor. It seems far more likely that Hague had gauged the relative strengths of the antagonists, concluded that Brandle was overmatched, and opted to bide his time while the conflict took its course. Once the viaduct was built and the contractors had moved on, a greatly humbled and far less powerful labor czar would be left for Hague to deal with.

Testimony by company officials shows that all four of the designated firms were aware of Teddy Brandle and his reputation as a labor czar before they began work. Curtis S. Garner, general manager of erection for American Bridge, framed the situation in an internal memorandum:

When this contract was let, we all knew there was going to be trouble in connection with labor, as there had been a good many threats made by labor leaders as to what they would do toward Open Shop contractors, so we began the operation with our eyes open, and we soon found out there would be trouble. . . . [T]hreats were made by Brandle, the local labor leader, that the American Bridge Company would never complete erection of this work and that tracks would be laid over certain streets over his dead body, etc. In view of these statements, the strength of the Union and what the labor leaders and Unions have done to other Open Shop contractors in Jersey City, we realized that protection had to be sought, as there was going to be a state of war against a peaceful corporation employing Jersey citizens in an Open Shop job.

The contractor's initial moves certainly seemed calculated to draw a line in the sand. The completion bond for the project was posted in cash, thereby denying Brandle's company hefty bonding fees. They also hired a New York–based security firm, Foster Industrial and Detective Agency, to guard the work site.

Along with the equipment needed to begin construction, the work site along the southern end of the Meadowlands was cordoned off with chain-link fencing and barbed wire. An elaborate plan for getting workers in and out of the area, to be used according to the intensity of the picketing, was already in place even before Brandle marshaled his forces.

Both sides were girding for war. But Brandle, for all his canniness in dealing with laborers and politicians, was about to go to war against a well-organized and highly experienced foe. He was outnumbered, outmanned, and outgunned, but he wouldn't realize it until too late.

CHAPTER 6

The War of the Meadows

What we are passing thru at Jersey City is practically a war condition. We must win, and no chances dare be taken.

—J. B. Gemberling, American Bridge Company, September 22, 1931

"I'll unionize this job or else!"

Teddy Brandle's threat, widely quoted in the *Jersey Journal* and other area newspapers, left the "or else" open to the imagination. Not that much imagination was needed. Each day, the work crews ran a gauntlet of seething, hard-eyed union men enraged by the presence of scabs. They watched, shouted, and threw things as the spring gave way to summer and the work crews prepared the ground for the immense highway in the sky that was about to be built.

Summer can be a remarkably miserable season in New Jersey, and on the tree expanse of the Meadowlands in South Kearny, the relentless heat and sun only amplified the misery. Angry men and angry workers eyed each other and exchanged barrages of thrown rocks as the thick, insect-laden air covered the ground like the hot breath from an open mouth.

There was remarkable work being done on the other side of the fence, and many of those union men must have yearned to

join it. All through the design of the Route 1 Extension, there
had been no question about the unsuitability of Meadowlands
mud for such a high-volume roadway. The road, designed to be
at grade all the way from Elizabeth to the edge of Newark,
would have to take to the air once it reached the swamp.

The Meadowlands are what remained after a huge glacier,
grinding away to the west of Bergen Hill and the Palisades,
carved out a basin and then retreated. (On the other side of the
ridge, another glacier carved out the path of the Hudson River,
pushing before it a terminal moraine of debris that would, over
the millennia, become Long Island.) The prehistoric muck, en-
riched with sediments streaming down from a good portion of
northern New Jersey, is well over a hundred feet deep in spots
and had to be carefully tested in order to locate the supporting
rock. Any construction would have to be supported by pilings,
driven deep.

The size and strength of the necessary support changed
when the War Department insisted on bridges that soared 135
feet above each of the rivers. Some of the big concrete piers
needed to hold the viaduct aloft could be supported by pilings,
while others had to be built on caissons. Fortunately, the huge
bunkers of the caissons could be sunk to the level of rock
through dredging under normal air pressure—no dangerous
sandhog work along the lines of the Holland Tunnel was
required.

Once the caissons were properly entombed in Meadowlands
mud, the concrete piers could rise from the swamp. The array
of digging and dredging techniques in use delighted the arm-
chair mechanics and technicians of the day, and *Scientific
American* took note of them in an admiring article. Civil engineers and professionals followed the work through journals
like *Engineering News-Record.* Pictures of the work site show

the white concrete forms emerging from the ground like bones in a titanic ossuary, arranged in neat formation.

And the men arrayed along the picket lines watched in steadily building frustration that rose along with the progress of the construction. For the sake of two dollars per day— twenty-five cents for each hour of a regular workday—they were barred from performing this work. From their side of the fence, the union men saw scabs willing to sell their brother workers down the river for a couple of dollars a day. From the other side, the nonunion workers saw thugs in the employ of a labor gangster.

The companies set the stage for the conflict by refusing even to consider negotiating with a union local. Their open-shop philosophy took away the one bargaining chip a union had: its ability to withhold the work of its members. This left the union members with an uncomfortable choice. They could slink away and starve virtuously, or they could take action. That was what fell under the heading of "or else." That was when the face-off turned into a game of chess. (There were seven labor spies in the union ranks who presumably passed along intelligence about Brandle's plans; what other role they may have played, perhaps as agents provocateurs in the confrontation, has never been established.) When the union men tried to make the work costlier by rushing the fence and wreaking havoc in the construction area, police and private guards held them back. When they tried to follow workmen to their cars and homes, the employers set up decoys. The rivers helped greatly: employees could be brought in from New York via boats, and when the fighting grew particularly intense, the employers floated in barges where the men could sleep.

The union men tried to circumvent these defenses. When they spotted boatloads of scabs coming in, they lined up along

McClintic-Marshall crews construct one of the bridges spanning the Hackensack and Passaic rivers along the route of the Pulaski Skyway.

the waterfront and pelted the boats with bolts and stones. (A plan by Brandle and his men to launch an interceptor boat was abandoned when it became clear that such a move would bring on federal involvement.) Any scab caught outside the perimeter, or recognized on the street, faced a terrible beating. Trucks bearing supplies to and from the Holland Tunnel would be cut off and harassed by chaser vehicles. Sometimes pickets managed to climb the fence and get into the work area. When that happened, days and weeks of accumulated rage would spur flying fists and stomping feet.

The viaduct work crews included a number of Mohawk Indian ironworkers from the Kahnawake tribal reservation on the south shore of the St. Lawrence River, in southern Quebec. That was and is the home of the "Iron Skywalkers," Mohawk steelworkers renowned for their seeming indifference to the danger of working on skyscrapers and bridges, boosted to near-legendary status by Joseph Mitchell and his famous essay, "The Mohawks in High Steel."

Ironically, the Mohawks probably wouldn't have had the chance to win this dashing image but for the Canadian government's habit of treating the forty-eight-square-mile reservation as a doormat—railways, power lines, and highways were all routed through Kahnawake, and the excavation of the St. Lawrence Seaway canal would sunder the Mohawks from their own river shoreline. Starting in the 1860s with the construction of the Victoria Bridge, Mohawks hired to run supplies to bridge construction sites demonstrated great aptitude and eagerness for walking along girders hundreds of feet in the air, and construction companies were quick to respond.

Though the Mohawks were willing to go "booming out" across the country in search of jobs, the abundance of work in the New York metropolitan area led to the establishment of a small Indian community in the Gowanus section of Brooklyn. Just about every skyscraper and bridge in and around New York was raised with the help of Mohawk hands, and in the War of the Meadows they shed blood and traded blows alongside Italian and Greek immigrants, second-generation Irish, and those who liked to think of themselves as natural-born Americans.

Once the piers were finished, the truly glorious work could begin. Rail tracks were laid down so traveling cranes could lift steel girders into position, where they could be riveted into place. The McClintic-Marshall bridge-building crews worked their way in from the opposite sides of each river, building the two halves of the arch along frames of wooden beams called "falsework," because to the casual spectator they gave the false impression of actually being the bridges. When the two halves of the arching bridge spans were complete, the falsework would be removed and the ends would settle together and meet at the high point—the "camber"—which would be made all the stronger by the pressure of their weight coming together.

Here the distractions of the labor war could become deadly. Steelwork at the time had an element of dangerous ballet. A workman manned a brazier, where rivets were heated to near white-hot consistency and then tossed aloft. The riveter's assistant, stationed above on a scaffolding, watched the tiny spark rising toward him, scooped it from the air with a bucket, and held it in place for the riveter, who shared his scaffold. The rivet gun smashed the near-molten rivet into the steel with a sound that seemed to pierce every organ and bone in a man's body. As the black steel framework of the viaduct took shape in the air, workmen entered an environment in which a moment's inattention could result in crippling, even fatal injury.

Men died building the Skyway—fourteen of them from work-related accidents. A riveter would lose his footing, or a man adjusting a scaffold would pull the wrong cord, and the result would be a quick plunge to the ground. It was roughly the same number of men that died during the construction of the George Washington Bridge, working at great height along the tall cliffs of the Palisades and the broad sweep of the Hudson River. Though safety nets would later be strung beneath large elevated structures during construction, no such niceties were available on the Meadowlands job.

Brandle's best shot at unionizing the viaduct project came on July 9, 1931, when 175 nonunion workers put down their tools and gathered to hear what the labor czar had to say. The crewmen, working at top speed in the swampy heat, had decided to halt work until they got the extra pay Brandle had been talking about. There were also worrisome rumors about a car with a mounted machine gun that was touring the lower Meadowlands, ready to pick off scab laborers. Jeffrey Reynolds, the superintendent of the McClintic-Marshall crew, told reporters there was no labor dispute, and that he'd called a halt to the job because he "did not like the looks of things."

According to the *Jersey Journal*, the employees gathered to hear Brandle speak from a platform, surrounded by a hundred union men. It was not an auspicious day: the platform started to collapse and the burly labor czar had to leap to safety.

The work stoppage lasted five days. Though they wanted more money, the crewmen resisted Brandle's call to join the union. The men finally dropped their demand for more money and returned to work on July 13 with their pay docked by three days. Ten of them quit outright, apparently frightened of Brandle's pickets. The returning workers entered the work site with help from a detachment of Kearny police. "Three days' pay lost by 155 men, and ten men thrown out of work because one man, reaching out for more power to bolster up his crumbling throne, sought to bring the iron workers under his domination!" the *Jersey Journal* thundered a few days later.

Did Brandle use thuggish tactics? Beyond a doubt. Did he live well off the dues paid by his men? Absolutely. But such editorials, even when they were accurate, got it wrong by telling only half the story. If there was exploitation, it went on from both sides of the fence. As to which chess player had the best interests of the men at heart—Teddy Brandle or his National Erectors' Association opponents—that is a question for posterity.

• • •

By the end of August 1931, the McClintic-Marshall crew had finished erecting the bridge over the Passaic River. Colonel H. W. Hudson from the state highway commission was on hand to watch the removal of the falsework and of the two five-hundred-ton hydraulic jacks that supported the spans. The two sides settled into place over the middle of the river and became a self-supporting unit. The completed bridge—arching over a river in the middle of nowhere, each side ending in midair with no connections—made for a surreal sight.

The *Newark Evening News* commemorated the August 27 milestone with a news item that reflected the conflicting emotions evoked by the pickets. There is, after all, no construction project as remarkable to the eye as a bridge job, and in the face of such an accomplishment, the reporter fell into a blatantly mocking tone as he contrasted the strong, taciturn bridge crewmen with the rabble of union picketers:

> A major phase of the battle of Newark meadows drew to a close today as workmen slipped floor beams into place after completing the steel span which is to carry State Highway 25 over the Passaic River a short distance north of the Lincoln Highway. The generals were saying nothing, saving breath for future engagements.
>
> Officials of the McClintic-Marshall Corporation, builders of the bridge, who were compelled to use the tactics of Swamp Fox Morgan in their battle with General Theodore M. Brandle of Hudson County, do not have to make comment. They point to the bridge.

Jeff Reynolds, the superintendent of construction, is described as "a large man with a broad, deep chest, a voice that makes the bullfrogs along the river quiet in envy, and iron gray hair." Taunts were duly recorded: "It is too bad this job was policed," one worker said. "We could have trimmed those picket boys five to one, and then there would not have been so much trouble." But the reporter saved the best bit for the end, blending macho strutting with a bit of racist hocus-pocus:

> The steel workers will finish their tasks in a few days. But even after they leave, there is one job growing out of the labor trouble which awaits James Nichobo, a worker who was beaten. He is an Indian. Police asked him to name his five assailants.
>
> "No," he said. "I do not need police to be revenged. I am an Indian. I handle my own affairs."
>
> And Indians never forget.

Under the circumstances, the reporter could be allowed a bit of jocularity. The labor war, while violent in terms of bruised faces, smashed fingers, and broken bones, had not yet cost any lives. It was a rough era. Policemen casually dangled nightsticks as they made their rounds, and in their role as keepers of the peace would frequently administer summary punishment to drunks and ne'er-do-wells. Bonnie and Clyde, the Barker-Karpis gang, and John Dillinger were ranging the Midwest, robbing banks and gas stations at will: Prohibition had turned gangsters into proto-folk heroes, inspiring fascination as well as fear, and the news was full of their murderous conflicts. Bloody clashes between police and union pickets were so frequent as to be scarcely newsworthy anymore. So—why not laugh the whole thing off? Nobody was getting hurt. Not really.

Two weeks after the Passaic River bridge was completed, representatives from the three major contractors—McClintic-

Marshall, American Bridge, and Phoenix Bridge—met at a Newark office to discuss getting a court injunction to stop the pickets. Curtis S. Garner, the general manager of erection on the American Bridge job, wrote a memo noting that the meeting was inconclusive, though it does offer some details about the size of the union picket groups. Garner wrote that

> there are from 50 to 350 pickets on the American Bridge Company job and probably from 50 to 100 on the jobs of the other companies—the American Bridge Company job being the most exposed one. . . . It is our duty to do everything within our power to relieve our superintendent and his organization at the site of the stress under which they are now working by having something done through an injunction or some other action to take away the pickets, but we must go slowly.

And so they did. The viaduct work was coming together nicely, despite the clashes and confrontations. The bridge companies, sworn enemies of unions, could take pride in demonstrating the utter impotence of the picketers.

The Kearny police arrayed outside the Meadowlands construction site were under orders to keep their nightsticks in their belts and their guns in their holsters. The "detectives" providing security within the perimeter were under no such constraints. So it seems only natural that the first shooting incident in the War of the Meadows involved a security guard firing at a picketer.

The shooting took place at about 10:30 a.m. on November 14, 1931. The union man was forty-seven-year-old Edward Bergin, who according to police was part of a mob of picketers throwing stones at workers on the American Bridge site in Jersey City, between Broadway and the Hackensack River. Bergin, who lived not far away on Neptune Avenue, later said he was there to check out the construction and collect some money he was owed by one of the picketers. Witnesses on the scene told police he was pitching stones alongside several other union men when security guard Ralph Golden, a thirty-year-old Bayonne resident, aimed his revolver and shot Bergin in the back, near his left shoulder. The sound of gunfire brought a Jersey City cop on the run, and he fired three shots into the air—a signal that brought every available patrolman flocking to the scene. Golden was arrested and charged with unlawful possession of a deadly weapon and assault with intent to kill. Another guard, thirty-year-old Harry Kelly of Bayonne, was arrested and charged with assault.

Bergin later recalled how it felt to lie facedown on the ground, arguing with the police about whether he'd been shot. The bullet had passed through his left shoulder blade, fractured an upper vertebra, and lodged somewhere in his right side. Both of his legs were paralyzed. Bergin, in shock from the wound, kept denying there was a problem until he was hoisted to his feet and allowed to fall to the ground. He was taken to the Jersey City Medical Center in a private car.

Shortly after the shooting, Patrick J. Hamill, a local physician working for the bridge companies, tried to get the details of Bergin's condition and was warned off by medical center executives. Three weeks later, he sent an assistant to scout out the terrain:

He very soon saw the reason for the warning given to me. The pickets were lining the corridors and watching who went in and out to see the patient. He was apparently or-

dered out, by whom I do not know, but he managed to re-
tire without having had any unpleasant experience. The
assumption of those in charge was that he was some insurance man and he is quite willing to let it go at that.

My friend, who is an executive officer in the hospital,
told me today that there are so many interests involved in
this particular case, and it is invested with such politico
labor influence, that a little caution in considering it
would be advisable. I reminded him that my interests lay
in the fact that I am a Steel Corporation surgeon but at
the same time many of the pickets had been patients of
mine, and as a matter of fact, the big fellow, our mutual
friend Teddy Brandle was never inimical to me. His exact
words to me following that were—"I understand that
just as well as you do, Doctor," and he said that "I am
pretty sure that in a case of any settlement you would be
more acceptable to Teddy than any other Doctor in the
city."

Hamill said Bergin exhibited "total paralysis of both legs
with paralysis of the bladder and rectum," which began to fade
after about ten days.

Bergin eventually regained the use of his legs, though he
had to keep them wrapped in bandages. His injury meant his
two daughters had to abandon their college plans and return
home. Later in life he would use crutches to get around, and
needed assistance from his wife when going to the toilet.

So, the first casualty of the war had been a union man. In a
few months, that balance would change.

In the predawn dark on the morning of February 27, McClintic-Marshall workman Byron Dickson started up his car and

began the drive south to the Meadowlands viaduct construction site. Riding with him were five other McClintic-Marshall workers: William T. Harrison, Gilbert Tolbott, Thomas Jones, W. D. Craven, and Garrett Stroup. The sun would probably have been starting to color the sky as they entered Jersey City and turned down Carlton Avenue.

A few blocks to the east, shadowy against the sky, loomed the girders of the Black Bridge—the span over the Erie Railroad tracks that would connect the Skyway to the depressed highway carved through Bergen Hill, and beyond it, the entrance to the Holland Tunnel. To the west, clearly visible beyond the rows of houses and vacant lots along Carlton Avenue, the steel latticework of the Hackensack River span would have been clearly visible, catching the first rays of the rising winter sun.

As the car neared Liberty Avenue, a man standing on the sidewalk turned and signaled with his newspaper. Two cars darted in from either side and blocked Dickson's way, forcing him to screech to a stop on the icy street. Instantly, the men inside Dickson's car were shouting in fear as a rain of bolts and rivets slammed into the car, turning the windows white with radiating cracks. Then shadows moved behind the whitened glass. A mob of about twenty men armed with iron bars smashed and thrust at the car, shattering all the glass remaining in the windows and shredding the roof. The clatter of metal on metal gave way to the thump of metal on flesh and bone as the six scabs tried to escape from the demolished vehicle.

A few houses down on Carlton Avenue, Jersey City police officer John A. McCarthy was jostled awake by his wife. "There's some trouble in the street," she said, then hurried to get his service revolver as he pulled on his trousers. McCarthy then ran out into the wintry street, barefoot, wearing only his trousers and a T-shirt, to see what was going on.

Amid the chaos of broken glass and spilled blood, McCarthy saw the shattered automobile. He also saw another man, this one holding an iron bar as he got into a car. McCarthy shoved his revolver in the man's face and herded him back across the street and into the vestibule of the McCarthy residence, where he kept the man under guard while his wife called the police. He was later identified as John J. Byrnes, thirty-six, of Weehawken, a gritty town perched on the cliffs just north of Hoboken.

A short distance away, William T. Harrison sat on the front steps of a house, clutching his head in agony. Someone had clubbed him with an iron bar, laying open a patch of skin and fracturing the man's skull. Harrison was rushed to the Jersey City Medical Center, where he languished through the evening. By the next morning, the father of two young children was dead.

Harrison's companions ran for their lives through the streets. Four took refuge in houses along Carlton Avenue. Craven limped across the frosty grass until he reached the McClintic-Marshall work site. Only Dickson refused medical aid, saying he was not injured.

Hague's reaction was swift and comprehensive. "Police were ordered today to wage relentless war against the Brandle gang-rioters," the *Jersey Journal* announced, adding that Hague had ordered the police to "disregard Brandle . . . or anybody else" as they pursued their investigation. Ironworkers were arrested seemingly at random, on no other evidence than that they were union members and had some fleeting connection with Teddy Brandle. By April 1932, police had rounded up or identified twenty-one ironworkers as suspects in the Harrison murder, some of whom had run off as far as Philadelphia to evade the Hague machine's dragnet. All were indicted April 15, though some remained to be rounded up.

One of the men arrested was William "Star" Campbell, twenty-two, an out-of-work prizefighter whose wife had recently died in childbirth at the Margaret Hague Maternity Hospital, leaving him with a large brood to feed. After his wife's death, Campbell had worked at a few odd jobs before Brandle's office offered him a chance to serve picket duty at the Meadowlands. Because of that, and apparently for no other reason, Campbell was snared in the police department's widely cast net.

Campbell would later testify that police subjected him to regular beatings at the jail until he agreed to sign a confession stating he had joined in beating Harrison. Whatever the truth of Campbell's testimony, what happened next is a matter of record. On a steaming hot July morning, after another period of contemplating his future as the target of Frank Hague's wrath—and what would become of his children after they lost their father once and for all—William "Star" Campbell slipped the belt off his raincoat and tried to hang himself in his jail cell. A guard spotted him dangling and rushed into the cell in time to save his life.

After a few days of treatment, Campbell was taken to the courthouse once again and formally charged with attempted suicide. There would be no way to escape the mayor, not even death.

CHAPTER 7

High, Wide, and Handsome

The whole enterprise [Route 1 Extension] is superhighway in
the fullest meaning of the term. . . . [I]t is a credit to the state
highway engineers and commissioners of New Jersey that in
meeting the problem which confronted them, they considered
no solution less than the best.

—Engineering News-Record (1930)

There are no words to describe that viaduct-highway, nor can it
be done even with pictures. It must be seen before one can realize its wonders. . . . Don't miss driving over that viaduct at
your earliest opportunity: it would be a pity to die before see-
ing it.

—Hudson Dispatch, editorial, November 23, 1932

By the fall of 1932, the diagonal highway—all 88,461 steely
black tons of it, goose-pimpled with over two million hand-
placed rivets—was nearly complete. The two bridge spans that
straddled the Hackensack and Passaic rivers were finally
joined by sections of roadway, after months of standing alone.
Drivers emerging from the depressed roadway through Bergen
Hill still faced time-consuming delays as they were funneled

down ramps at Broadway and the Tonnele Circle, but they could see the future stretching away into the distance just before they made their descent.

The fourteenth and last workman to die on the project was Christi Theodarokis, a forty-year-old Greek émigré who lived in New York City. Theodarokis, married and the father of three children, spent the day applying black paint to the steel structure above Kearny. Late in the afternoon, Theodarokis started to adjust the level of the scaffold he shared with another painter, only to slip and plunge seventy-five feet to the ground. The other worker, Just Muginis—who, like Theodarokis, lived on Madison Street—clung to the scaffold's safety wire. He remained there, immobilized by terror, staring down at the shattered body of his neighbor and co-worker, until other workmen lowered a cable and hoisted him away from danger.

Teddy Brandle had made his final plea for peace with Hague, only to be left holding his hat at City Hall. Brandle's personal fortune was dwindling: no more state business was being channeled through his bonding company, the union locals he controlled were openly restive, and he was hemorrhaging money paying the legal costs of his men. The newspapers were already referring to the War of the Meadows the way they might have referred to the Peloponnesian War—a thing of the distant past.

The wish to move on was only natural: signs of progress were to be seen everywhere in the region, whether in the air or beneath the ground. The sky was crisscrossed by buzzing propeller-driven airplanes: Newark Metropolitan Airport, the first major airport in the New York area, had opened in October 1928, several months after the Newark city fathers had designated sixty-eight acres of Meadowlands muck for development as an airport and dedicated $5.5 million to pay for the

work. It was already one of the busiest airports in the world—
in its first full year of operation, over four thousand passenger
planes lifted off from Newark's cinder-strip runways, and by
the time the Meadowlands viaduct was finished, the airport
saw over 150 flights a day. Meanwhile, portions of the obsolete
Morris Canal were being drained and adapted to create
Newark's first subway system.

Along the eastern horizon, the distant spire of the Empire
State Building—completed a year earlier and still mostly
empty of tenants—poked up through the haze above the
traprock ridge. (Work had already started on the foundations of
that other Midtown Manhattan icon, Rockefeller Center.) Several miles north, lost to sight, the steel tracery of the George
Washington Bridge—also completed the year before—
spanned the windy gap of the Hudson River between Fort Lee,
New Jersey, and Manhattan's Fort Washington Park. The
George Washington Bridge and its cousin, the single-arched
Bayonne Bridge across the brackish waters of the Kill Van
Kull, had opened within weeks of each other in late 1931. In
another two years the Lincoln Tunnel would provide the final
automobile link between Manhattan and New Jersey—Weehawken, to be precise. Not long afterward, the complex of
spans called the Triborough Bridge would cross the waterways
of New York City to knit together Manhattan, Queens, and the
Bronx.

Though the South Kearny area would eventually be choked
with warehouses, truck farms, and junkyards, the sparsely developed landscape that existed in 1932 offered a vista of almost
surrealistic contrasts: the southern extreme of the Meadowlands, bright with swamp grasses and weeds or smeared with
mud and dusty roads, dotted with hobo shanties and farms to
the north; the hulking mass of the Public Service generator

building, with its four smokestacks and incongruously decorative cathedral windows; the low skyline of Newark and the
teeming shipyards along Newark Bay and Kearny to the west;
the dreamy silhouette of the Empire State Building to the east;
factories and warehouses lining the waterfront to the immediate south, where the gunmetal gray waters of the Hackensack
and Passaic rivers poured into Newark Bay.

And running through the middle of it was the new viaduct.
It was a long black framework of angled beams—brute
strength assembled into an oddly graceful line. Photographs
taken in the weeks before the grand opening show the road itself wide open and bright in the sun, without the aluminum
divider that would have to be installed in later years. One
newspaper picture shows five of the era's boxy automobiles,
shadowy lumps against the white concrete, lined shoulder to
shoulder across the elevated highway—a vision of expansive
comfort and convenience for local residents who had spent accumulated months of their lives stalled in long lines along the
narrow roads across the huge swamp.

H. W. Hudson, the last of the daisy chain of engineers involved on the project, personally drove back and forth along
the black steel viaduct to gauge the amount of time drivers
would save. Driving at the posted speed limit—probably the
first and last time anyone would do so—Hudson found that a
drive from Newark Airport to Times Square was a mere thirty
minutes, while the drive from the airport to New York City
Hall could be wrapped up in twenty-five minutes.

At a time when much of the population could remember a
landscape of dirt roads and horse-drawn buggies, the black
steel arm of the viaduct must have seemed like the physical
manifestation of the future, reaching out to bind Newark and
Jersey City and haul both of them into the modern age. The

opening of the viaduct would be timed for the Thanksgiving holiday, with Mayor Frank Hague to preside over the ceremony, and the citizenry would be encouraged to give thanks for what human ingenuity wedded to government largesse had been able to accomplish.

It was good to have something to celebrate. The year 1932 had been a mean, poisonous time for the country, and people would welcome any opportunity to look ahead to the good things the future would bring—would *have* to bring.

To understand the viciousness of the Skyway labor war, it helps to remember the sheer desperation and simmering violence of the time. The broiling summer of 1932 had seen the arrival of the Bonus Expeditionary Force, a ragged gathering of over twenty-five thousand veterans of the Great War with their wives and children in Washington, D.C. They had braved poison gas and the mechanized slaughter of the trenches to face down the Hun, and in 1924 a grateful Congress approved the Adjusted Compensation Act, which would give the surviving veterans a large cash payment in 1945. The marchers had calculated that early payment would mean about five hundred dollars for each of them—a small fortune and a literal lifesaver as the country staggered through the second year of the Great Depression with no relief in sight. In May of 1932, they gathered from all over the country to petition Congress for that payment.

The marchers established several squatter villages throughout the city, but the largest camp was in Anacostia Flats, across the river from the Capitol. Already starved scarecrow-thin, the veterans lived in a riot of tents, abandoned automobiles, and shacks hammered together from chicken coops and discarded lumber. The veterans were careful to eject any radicals or

Communists from their ranks; they marched up and down Pennsylvania Avenue in faded uniforms, and waited for word from their government. Congress adjourned for the summer without taking action; President Hoover called them Reds and ordered the gates of the Executive Mansion chained shut, then had all traffic barred within a block of the White House. Tormented by insects and the swampy heat, the veterans waited to see if Hoover would receive a delegation of their leaders.

Hoover's answer came on July 28 and was delivered by a four-star general named Douglas MacArthur, commanding a force that included George S. Patton and Dwight D. Eisenhower. Coming in on a wave of tear-gas bombs, soldiers routed the marchers and set fire to their camps. Some marchers tried to fight back, but all they had were rocks and clubs. William J. Haska, a destitute marcher from Chicago, was shot dead in one of the clashes and buried a few days later in Arlington National Cemetery—with an honor guard that doubtless included some of the same soldiers who'd chased the marchers from the city's parks.

Among American presidents, Herbert Hoover is somewhat underrated. Though the philosophy of limiting government action was knit into his very bones, he had responded to the Depression by creating the Reconstruction Finance Company and authorizing it to spend hundreds of millions of dollars on relief, and well over a billion for public improvements. The RFC would be the cornerstone finance agency of the coming New Deal. But the photographs of American veterans and their families running from the bayonets of American soldiers, with the Capitol dome framed by the smoke from their burning encampment, sent a wave of disgust through the country. Hoover, with his obvious distaste for the masses and his penchant for sour, ill-timed witticisms—he once suggested that many of the nation's jobless men had deliberately chosen apple selling as a more lucrative alternative—guaranteed that the feeling would linger through November, when voters swept him from office.

As the last chores of the Meadowlands viaduct project were completed, Hague pondered what sort of show he would arrange to herald the Thanksgiving opening of the new elevated highway. Hague was a man with his own reasons to be thankful. Only about three months earlier, Hague had rallied the Hudson County faithful for a spectacle that saved his political neck, and guaranteed the continued prosperity of his organization. It had also ended one of his oldest friendships and bound his fortunes to a man who considered him one of the lowest of the low, a jackal in spats and homburg, but Hague was nothing if not pragmatic about such matters.

As the Depression continued to choke off citizens' hopes, Democrats in general—and Al Smith in particular—knew they were going to win big. Herbert Hoover's platitudes about prosperity being just around the corner were a bitter national joke. Hobo villages along railroad tracks were becoming known as Hoovervilles; jackrabbits caught for the communal cook pot were called Hoover hogs. The very language of America was turning against the Republicans.

The Happy Warrior, still rankled by the barrage of anti-Catholic and anti-Irish bigotry he had endured in the 1928 campaign against Hoover, was eager to win vindication. Though Smith had indicated he would not make another run, he reversed course and announced his candidacy for the Democratic presidential nomination in January. His old friend and ally, Frank Hague, once again did his part by trying to neutralize Franklin Delano Roosevelt's steadily building momentum.

During the run-up to the 1932 Democratic national convention in Chicago, where he was to serve as a vice chairman and a floor manager for Smith, Hague made a pilgrimage to the city to argue Smith's case (unsuccessfully) with political boss Anton Cermak, the mayor of Chicago. Hague spent another few weeks rallying anti-Roosevelt delegates in the Middle Atlantic states. He then caught a train to Chicago a few days before the convention opened, and on June 23 released a statement to the press warning that Roosevelt "cannot carry a single state east of the Mississippi and very few in the Far West." He even warned that New Jersey could very well go Republican again if FDR won the Democratic nomination.

With a friend like Hague, Smith had considerably less need for enemies. From the viewpoint of many delegates, Hague's use of his convention position as a bully pulpit for Smith was distasteful; his warning that New Jersey might tip to the GOP was seen as a veiled threat—downright treasonous coming from a man whose mastery of Garden State elections was already the stuff of legend. Hague worked around the clock against Roosevelt, and just about every delegate in Chicago must have felt that famous index finger poking his chest.

True to his friendship, Hague kept New Jersey's thirty-six votes in the Smith line right up to the last round of voting, long after it became clear that Roosevelt had swept the field. During the glum train ride home, Hague contemplated a political universe in which he, a Democrat, would have no strings to pull with a Democrat in the White House: a universe, moreover, in which he would be persona non grata while federal patronage was divvied up. Crossing the Meadowlands by rail, less than a mile from the place where the future Skyway was taking shape, Hague considered his chances with a candidate whose attitude toward political bosses ranged from ambiguous to hostile. As a young state senator in New York, Roosevelt had called Tammany Hall's sachems "beasts of prey"—what if he decided to grace New Jersey with an ambitious U.S. attorney eager to start digging in Hudson County?

Since Hague was not a man to keep a diary or a journal, we don't know how his dark night of the soul played out. We do know that on July 11 he stood before the Hudson County Democratic Committee and publicly announced his support for the man he had previously warned would lose half the continental United States if nominated. He also tracked down James Farley, Roosevelt's campaign manager and future postmaster general, who had gone to Atlantic City to decompress after the bruising primary and convention fight. Farley had barely dipped his toes in the surf when he found himself taking a phone call from his former nemesis, who promised that if Roosevelt officially kicked off his presidential campaign in New Jersey, he—Frank Hague—would make the announcement the centerpiece of the biggest political rally anyone had seen.

And so it came to pass that on August 27, Franklin Delano Roosevelt traveled to the Jersey Shore town of Sea Girt, where he made the first speech of his presidential campaign with the ocean at his back and a sea of sun hats and straw boaters before him. The Hudson County Democratic organization did itself proud, chartering trains and commissioning box lunches and entertainment for party loyalists, curiosity seekers, and anyone with a pulse who was willing to sit in a hot rail car for the slow grind to the Jersey Shore. "Frank Hague kept his word," Farley later wrote:

It was a lovely summer day, although a bit hot, and a flat field of many acres stretched out in front of the speakers' platform every square foot of which seemed to be filled up with people. They were standing up, packed tightly together in solid ranks, and at first glance the crowd seemed endless. While it is very nearly an impossible task to estimate the size of a crowd like that, the chances are that the newspaper estimates, which varied from 100,000 to 115,000 people, were not far wrong. Certainly the throng was vast enough to cover the playing field of a couple of major league ball parks. If it wasn't the biggest rally in history up to that time, it must have been very close to it.

Gazing out over this cheering and whooping crowd, Roosevelt saw a promise kept and a warning not too subtly delivered. Hague may have been licked in Illinois, but he was still a king in New Jersey, and no Democrat could afford to write off the voting bloc that Hague rallied at will. The boss of Hudson County kept his promise—his support for Roosevelt never wavered, and when Hoover was swept from office by a wave of Democratic votes, Hague marked the occasion with a victory rally that packed Journal Square with cheering crowds.

Though he personally despised Hague, Roosevelt never moved against him openly, and he allowed the Boss to skim a portion of the salaries paid to workmen on the Works Progress Administration projects that were lavished on Hudson County. It was the sweetest, richest rice pudding of all, and it nourished the Hague organization all through the lean years of the Depression—years that might otherwise have crippled the machine, or even killed it.

Whenever humanity's technical ingenuity bridges great distances, the natural impulse is to celebrate the accomplishment. For reasons both primal and practical, the symbolism of the celebration is often bound up in oceanic imagery, as though the immense natural power of the sea—that immovable barrier that remained unconquered even as the land was tilled and developed—had been tapped. When the Erie Canal opened in 1825, New York governor De Witt Clinton boarded a packet boat in Buffalo and sailed east along the canal's entire 363-mile length with two casks of fresh water scooped from Lake Erie; upon reaching New York City, he emptied the casks into New York Harbor and declared "the marriage of the waters." In the early days of cross-country motoring, drivers would baptize their vehicles' tires with water from the Atlantic Ocean, then reprise the ceremony once they reached the Pacific. The impulse extends to communication as well as transportation. When the news series *See It Now* premiered in 1951 on CBS-TV, the November 18 broadcast treated viewers across the country to simultaneous views of the Pacific and Atlantic oceans—a technical feat made possible only by freshly laid coaxial cable.

So it seems only natural that on the day before Thanksgiving, the dedication ceremony for the Meadowlands viaduct—the last link in the transit chain that helped pull together America's first cross-country highway—included a baptism with waters from both the Atlantic and Pacific oceans, which arrived by plane at the Newark Metropolitan Airport. Airplanes crisscrossed the sky above the viaduct, and the Meadowlands—a barrier to travel and commerce for hundreds of years—began to look rather small and inconsequential.

Podiums draped with bunting were set up at either end of the black steel behemoth and at the Kearny access ramp. Over 2,500 attendees gathered to hear a band concert and speeches from Hague; General Hugh L. Scott, chairman of the New Jersey Highway Commission; the current governor, A. Harry

This editorial-page cartoon from the *Hudson Dispatch*
gives an idea of the general euphoria accompanying
the opening of the Meadowlands viaduct. Though the
cartoonist appears to have wished the town of Kearny
out of existence, his estimate of the time savings for
drivers between Jersey City and Newark was correct.

Moore; and his two predecessors, Morgan Larson and George
Silzer, men of different parties who owed their terms as governor to Hague's strategic planning.

It was a crowded agenda but the event moved along briskly,
goosed by the icy winds knifing across the frozen Meadowlands. "If Alexander Hamilton were here today," Moore
cracked, "he'd say it's a mighty cold day." The dignitaries then
hustled into a small fleet of cars, which bore them east to Jersey City, and then west to Newark.

Every regional newspaper covered the event and did its best to pump up anticipation of the official opening on Thanksgiving morning. The *Hudson Dispatch* proclaimed TOMORROW YOU'LL BE RIDING HIGH, WIDE AND HANDSOME, and ran a fawning editorial cartoon in which a bearded giant representing New Jersey straddled an expanse of water between Newark and Jersey City (Kearny having suddenly gone missing), set down a bridge, and, with a genial smile, said, "Now they are only five minutes apart." The newspaper editorial staff urged drivers to traverse the highway as soon as possible, while they were still young enough to savor its wonders. The *Newark Evening News,* harkening back to the early 1800s and the stagecoaches operated by Newark entrepreneur Thomas Watkins, announced: MR. WATKINS WOULD BE VERY MUCH SURPRISED.

The Meadowlands viaduct formally opened to traffic at 8 a.m. on Thanksgiving, and the first day was a microcosm of the span's future statistics. There were drivers from all over the region: Harry R. C. Hickey of Brooklyn, the first motorist to travel west; Murray Wennerholm of North Bergen, New Jersey, the first to travel east. There were speeders: the first traffic ticket was issued to Henry Becque of Dunellen, New Jersey, for driving fifty-five miles per hour in a forty-mile-per-hour zone. There was heavy traffic volume: by midnight, according to police, some forty-nine thousand cars—fifty-two vehicles a minute—had traveled the viaduct. There had even been a traffic jam, caused when a motorist ran out of gas on one of the viaduct's steep grades. And according to Frances Oakley, who was one of many Jersey City residents eager to try out the new thoroughfare, there was an injury—a city police officer was struck by a passing car during a traffic stop. All harbingers of things to come.

It was quite a day for Hudson County, and quite a year for Frank Hague. The labor war that had marred the construction of the viaduct was noted only fleetingly, if at all, in much of the press coverage. But it certainly must have been on Hague's mind. The Meadowlands murder trial was only weeks away; Teddy Brandle was on the ropes and ready to drop. And the crusade that would mark a whole new phase of Hague's political reign was about to begin.

CHAPTER 8

The Nightstick Must Prevail

Gentlemen, we stopped them [the CIO]. Not only did we stop
them, but we locked them up. As long as I am mayor of this city
the great industries are secure. We hear about constitutional
rights, free speech and the free press. Every time I hear these
words I say to myself, "That man is a Red, that man is a Com-
munist." You never heard a real American talk in that manner.

—Frank Hague, speech before Jersey City Chamber of Commerce,
April 2, 1938

One of the shocks [I learned] was the totality of Hague's
power. In the Western Union office in Journal Square, a police
lieutenant read every telegram that came in and out of the city
each day. Anyone who deposited more than $7,000 in a local
bank was liable to be invited to City Hall to explain where he
got the money. Phones were, of course, tapped whenever the
mayor considered it necessary. Along with fear there was the
constant use of favor. If a critic could not be intimidated, his
loyalty could often be bought with a good job.

—Thomas Fleming, *Mysteries of My Father*

Two weeks after traffic began to pour across the Meadowlands viaduct, the twenty-one men accused of murdering

William T. Harrison were herded into a Jersey City courtroom packed with family members and spectators. There, on Tuesday morning, December 6, they found Hudson County prosecutor John Drewen awaiting them with a table display of rivets, bolts, and iron bars—weapons, Drewen told the court, harvested from the bloody street where Harrison and his five companions had been attacked.

Three attorneys represented the accused union men: George E. Cutley, Saul Nemser, and John J. Carlin. Sitting with them at the defense table, where he would remain throughout the trial, was Teddy Brandle, dapper as always. His personal fortune had already been drastically reduced by the expense of the picketing and medical care for his men, but if the prospect of bankruptcy caused him any distress, Brandle didn't show it in the courtroom.

The trial was held in the Court of Oyer and Terminer, at that time the name for a general criminal court. (The antique term *oyer and terminer*, meaning "hear to the end," was one of a welter of confusing court jurisdictions mandated in New Jersey's nineteenth-century constitution; it was eliminated when the state constitution was overhauled in the 1940s.) The court had authorized night sessions to allow for additional testimony in what everyone assumed would be a lengthy trial—two weeks, possibly more. After years of rioting and shooting, it could certainly be expected that the trial would take weeks to sort everything out.

Certainly nobody expected what actually did happen.

The first sign that Drewen's case against the ironworkers was a little less than airtight came right at the start of the trial, when the indictments against ten defendants were dismissed. Another three were turned loose just before the prosecutor and the defense made their closing statements. The trial that was supposed to last for weeks was wrapped up after two days of testimony and a third day mostly spent waiting for the jurors to render their finding.

Drewen deployed a total of thirty-one witnesses, including Vincent Albano, a Foster agency detective who claimed to have overheard defendant Charles "Red" Ackerman and other union men bragging about the attack in a local restaurant on the morning of the Harrison murder. "We sent a dozen snakes to the hospital," Ackerman said, according to the detective, "and you better all duck and we will call it a day."

Albano's testimony was overshadowed, however, by William "Star" Campbell, who took the stand after Drewen introduced into evidence a signed statement from Campbell admitting to having taken part in the attack on Harrison and his companions. Campbell told the court he had endured several days of beatings and abuse from the Jersey City police, a situation so extreme that he finally tried to kill himself in his jail cell. He had finally signed the confession in order to end the pain.

Drewen's arsenal of signed affidavits from witnesses claiming to have seen the defendants at the scene of the attack rapidly became an embarrassment as one witness after another disowned the testimony, saying they had been pressured by the police or by Drewen himself. Robert Orr, a neighborhood resident, told the court he'd signed his affidavit only when Drewen threatened to prosecute him as an accessory to murder.

"Orr was on the verge of collapsing on the stand," the *Newark Evening News* reported. "He constantly wiped his face with a handkerchief and at one point he had to be refreshed by a drink of water."

"You cross-questioned me in your office and harassed me until I did not know if I was sitting or standing and told me as

The Passaic River span of the Pulaski Skyway shortly after its completion in 1932, when the route was still known as the High-Level Viaduct.

a prosecutor that I could be held for aiding and abetting this murder," Orr said. The jury watched as Drewen gave Orr a chance to compose himself, then asked the judge's indulgence as he slowly led Orr back through his testimony and finally got him to admit that the version of events given to Drewen "might be the correct one." The judge pitched in by loudly praising Drewen's courage and integrity before the court.

The prosecutor's summation took about an hour. "Don't get the idea in your heads that the state seeks blood or vengeance," Drewen told the jury. Twice during his speech, Drewen hefted an iron bar and let it crash to the floor, jolting the entire courtroom. When he read lengthy excerpts from Campbell's confession, the ironworker shouted, "That's a lie!" in a hoarse voice. Drewen also noted that several of the defendants had been caught after fleeing the city; many had not even been willing to testify on their own behalf.

"You can't go on in that manner and have a progressive eco-

nomic civilization," Drewen declared, ending his summation
on a less than overwhelming note.

As George Cutley rose to present the defense summation, it
was clear that Drewen had not been able to place the defendants at the scene. It is the measure of Cutley's confidence that
the testimony of defense witnesses took up barely a half hour
of court time, and his summation was equally terse. He
ridiculed Albano's testimony, noted that the hysterical atmosphere of the time had led some of his clients to flee, and supported the decision not to have most of the defendants speak
before the jury. "All the evidence existing in the world is before
you," Cutley told the jury.

After a few hours behind closed doors, the jurors emerged.
All eight defendants were found to be "not guilty." Pandemo-
nium filled the courtroom as the defendants and their families
cried out in joy. For all the posturing and speech making, for all
the strong-arm tactics by the police, the Hague machine had
not been able to bag a single man.

The *Hudson Dispatch*, always quick with a superlative when
one of Hague's men was involved, said, "Prosecutor Drewen's
summation was regarded as a classic by lawyers in the courtroom," then noted lower down in the story that even the prosecutor admitted "there was very little evidence" to convict the
men. This left readers to wonder which attorney, aside from
Drewen himself, might have thought so highly of the summation.

The *Newark Evening News*, safely located on the other end
of the Skyway, was guarded but far less sycophantic. "While it
was not felt by those who followed the testimony that Prosecutor Drewen had made a case warranting a verdict of first degree murder," the uncredited story said, "verdicts of second
degree murder or manslaughter against two or three of the

men and assault and battery against several others had been anticipated."

Either way, nothing of the sort had happened. Since Drewen was not even present for the reading of the verdict, it can only be assumed that he knew the cause was lost. Judge Brown acted like a man displeased with the outcome: after barking at the overjoyed defendants and their families to keep quiet, Brown curtly dismissed the jurors without even offering the customary thanks to people who have taken time to render unpaid public service.

Cutley had swept the field. In a city where Hague wielded nearly complete control over the police and judiciary, where even ordinary citizens not on the machine payroll thought twice before contradicting City Hall, Cutley had rescued twenty-one lost souls from the wrath of the Boss—rescued most of them, in fact, without even going before the jury.

If the Skyway murder trial hadn't been completely overshadowed by the Lindbergh kidnapping case, George Cutley would probably be at least as well known as William Kunstler or other examples of that much maligned, little appreciated breed—the topflight defense lawyer who represents the defendants everyone "knows" are guilty, until it turns out they're not.

Nevertheless, Cutley's credentials as a lawyer for the underdog were well established. Three years later, when Bruno Richard Hauptmann was tried and convicted for the kidnapping and death of Charles A. Lindbergh Jr., Cutley was one of the attorneys Anna Hauptmann consulted during the appeals of her husband's death sentence.

Star Campbell and the other ironworkers returned to homes where family life had been damaged by the incarceration of the family breadwinner, and to neighborhoods where Hague and his men had denounced them as murderers. And William

T. Harrison, family man and faithful provider, went un-avenged. His murderer was never identified, and the investigation was apparently abandoned. The case, having failed to yield the desired political result, would never be solved. Harrison was twice victimized: first by a thug with an iron bar, then again by another thug—a mayor who controlled the resources of an entire city, and who had the power to turn Harrison's murder into a political circus, but had no interest in solving it.

When the trial started, Frank Hague, clearly anticipating a long series of hearings in which Brandle and his union men would be dragged through the dirt in proper headline-grabbing style, formally launched his war against "gorilla labor leaders" and "labor racketeers." Though he didn't get to start his war with twenty-one union heads mounted on his wall, Hague went at it with all rhetorical guns blazing. After a decade of close association with Brandle and other labor bosses in the American Federation of Labor, Hague had suddenly discovered "sabotage, double dealing, brutality, terrorism, intimidation, exploitation, and gorilla-rule" associated with some of the Hudson County unions:

> I am determined to end it, irrespective of who may be the victim. I'm serving notice on every labor racketeer in this town that I am going to put an end to the rule of the iron bar and gas pipe. If necessary we'll match night-sticks against gas-pipes, but the gas-pipes are not going to enforce a rule of terror while I'm mayor of this city.

Later, as though he needed to emphasize the point, Hague told the *New York Times* that in any confrontation between labor leaders and the Jersey City police, "the nightstick must prevail." The *Newark Evening News* was only too happy to join in:

> Newark and its neighbors have suffered incalculably from these extortions and it has been hard, indeed, to break down the power of the "leaders" and to make all the rank and file see that they have been exploited. Hague's break with "Czar" Brandle of the building trades was the signal for extending the fight being made here into the labor stronghold of Hudson. Mr. Hague knows how to fight these gentry, as has been shown by the fashion in which his police department cleared Jersey City of the gangsters who have found Newark to be such a comfortable place. Hague will use no cologne water and he will fight the racketeers in the only way they should be fought—ruthlessly and without getting too touchy about the constitutional rights of manipulators who wouldn't know the Constitution if they saw it.

The notion of praising Frank Hague—the man whose walk-in vault absorbed thousands of dollars every month from numbers runners and bookies, friend to the Big Bankroll and a man who served Longy Zwillman's illegal hooch to guests—as the scourge of gangsters in Jersey City must have caused a great deal of merriment on the city desk, but then the *Newark Evening News* wouldn't have been the first or the last newspaper in which the editorial writers and the news writers seemed to exist in separate universes. As it was, the editorialist could apparently keep a straight face while claiming the racketeers had driven industries from Jersey City and Newark, despite the fact that Jersey City was already legendary as a town where the property tax levies—necessary to support the voracious machine Hague had built—were among the highest in the nation.

As it turned out, nightsticks were the least of the weapons at Duh Mare's command. His domination of the state court system allowed him to force union locals into receiverships, where a court-appointed master would oversee the local's affairs and drain its finances until it was helpless, or compliant enough to be released. Hague also pulled his strings with the governor to get the state Chancery Court to issue injunctions against strikers and pickets. And he gave his police full authority to harass and arrest any suspicious or undesirable characters spotted in the city.

Ironworkers Local 45, not surprisingly, was the first local placed into receivership. Hague quietly ordered one of his appointees in Chancery Court, Vice Chancellor John J. Fallon, to issue a writ against the local in January 1933. The writ appointed John Lenehan, a police justice and one of Hague's closest associates, to take control of the local as temporary receiver.

Everything was done on the q.t. to keep from alerting Brandle, but the labor czar was no fool, and when Lenehan arrived at the local's weekly meeting with a phalanx of city police, ready to seize the local's business records, he found only jeering union men and a business office devoid of any records except a list of dues-paying members. Lenehan went back to City Hall with egg on his face, but this was a war of attrition, and time was on his side. The coming year would be a cascade of bad news for Teddy Brandle, whose empire was crumbling under the hammer blows of Hague's war and the economic losses from the Depression.

In the case of the ironworkers, Hague's crusade was made easier by the fact that Brandle was genuinely unpopular with many of the workers. Robert Fleming, a Jersey City iron-worker, remembered hearing his grandfather—who had worked under Brandle's reign—complaining about the labor czar's autocratic style. The rank and file had been particularly irked by Brandle's summary dismissal of an offer to join forces with a north Jersey millworkers union, a team-up the iron-workers saw as a way to increase their clout. Perhaps Brandle, who was already wearing about a dozen hats by that point, was worried about stretching himself too thin.

If so, he would quickly find his schedule drastically reduced. In March 1933, the members of Local 45—which had already been placed in receivership—voted 359 to 1 to "accept Brandle's resignation." In June 1933, at a meeting of the ironworkers union general executive board in St. Louis, Missouri, Brandle and his four closest union associates were formally stripped of their titles on the charge that they had misused their titles. When John O'Neill was formally inducted as business agent of Local 45 in March 1934, the *New York Times* announced: BRANDLE LABOR RULE IS ENDED IN NEW JERSEY. He resigned two months later from his post as head of the New Jersey State Building Trades Council. The council members completed the work of eliminating Brandle's influence later that month by voting in a slate of anti-Brandle executives at the council's convention in Atlantic City. The Union Labor Investment Corporation, which controlled the Labor National Bank, filed for bankruptcy that summer. Brandle's legal troubles would continue through the decade, until Brandle and four executives of the defunct Union Labor Investment Corporation were ordered to pay the successor corporation $34,250 to reimburse loans that had been approved illegally.

By this point, Hague's antilabor crusade was well under way. Another Hague man, N. Louis Paladeau Jr., was appointed re-

ceiver of Local 274 of the United Association of Journeymen
Plumbers and Steamfitters in February 1933. When a group of
cleaners and dyers prepared to join Teamsters Local 617, police
swept down on the head of the local, Jeremiah Buckley, in June
and charged him with "obtaining money under false pre-
tenses." Two Teamsters locals were placed into receivership
and released only after the locals agreed to oust Buckley and
his associates.

While this offensive continued against other locals, police
were allowed to decide for themselves if a union picket line
was a threat to public order, and summarily arrest dozens of
picketers at a sweep. Judges would then dispense one-, two-,
and three-month jail sentences to picketers on an almost
whimsical basis.

During one of these picket cases in Chancery Court, Vice
Chancellor Maja Berry formulated the novel theory that free
speech was only a privilege granted by the Constitution,
whereas the property rights of employers were "natural and
inalienable rights." In a conflict between the two—when striking employees, for example, wanted to picket a store against
the owner's wishes—free speech would always have to yield
before property rights. The challenge to this notion of justice
would come in a few years, when a fledgling labor group called
the Congress of Industrial Organizations decided to storm the
antilabor fortress that Jersey City had become.

The CIO had already enjoyed success in organizing workers
elsewhere in New Jersey, but in Hoboken and Jersey City its
members had long been arrested, harassed, and summarily
ejected. Unlike the American Federation of Labor, which represented only crafts unions and disdained unskilled labor, the
CIO had been formed specifically to organize the kind of

sweatshop employees that were becoming the mainstay of Jersey City's economy. New Jersey's regional CIO director, John Carney, began laying his plans in November 1937, and on November 22 he announced that CIO organizers would visit Jersey City en masse to distribute flyers informing workers of their rights under the 1935 Labor Relations Act. "Hague may be the law in Jersey City," Carney said, "but he is not the law of the country."

City police were stationed at all entry points to Jersey City, particularly the Hudson Tubes. CIO workers were arrested as they arrived and thrown back onto ferries bound for Manhattan, or crammed into vans and abruptly dropped in Kearny and Harrison, or simply dumped in the Meadowlands. Those who managed to slip past the cordon sanitaire were rounded up later.

If Jersey City had previously been mocked as a proto–police state, it developed the characteristics of a real one during Hague's battle with the CIO. Random searches and arrests became commonplace. A police officer monitored all telegrams coming through the Western Union office in Journal Square. Incoming mail was routinely opened and studied for signs of union activity; when word got back to James Farley, FDR's postmaster general, Farley erupted in fury and told the president he wanted to file felony charges against Hague. "You go tell Frank to knock it off," Roosevelt told him. "We can't have this kind of thing going on. But keep this quiet. We need Hague's support if we want New Jersey." The Boss's political clout was enough to cow even the president.

The CIO continued to work to organize Jersey City workers, and the cat-and-mouse game extended into 1938. Hague denounced the CIO as a cabal of Communists, and forbade the group to speak anywhere in his city. This prompted Socialist leader Norman Thomas to announce during his afternoon May Day speech in Manhattan that he would travel to Journal Square that night to make an impromptu speech. When he arrived by car a few hours later, Jersey City police pounced on Thomas and dumped him onto the Pavonia Ferry bound for Manhattan. Though the *New York Daily News* and other papers frankly reported the incident as a kidnapping, FBI head J. Edgar Hoover evidently felt no need to pursue an investigation, since Thomas had not been imprisoned.

Undaunted, Thomas announced that he would hold a June 4 rally across the Skyway in Newark's Military Park, highlighted by a speech called "The Role of Hagueism in New Jersey." Hague lobbied to get Thomas's speaking permit rescinded. When that didn't work, he reached out to his gangster buddy, Longy Zwillman, and asked him to do something about it.

The June 4 rally began as planned with a crowd of about two hundred onlookers, but the Saturday night affair turned into a rout as a twenty-five-piece American Legion brass band entered the park and faced Thomas from the foot of the stage, blaring out patriotic songs whenever he tried to speak. Then a group of Minutemen, local bruisers employed by Zwillman as strikebreakers and hired muscle, began pelting Thomas with eggs and tomatoes. A newspaper photographer caught an image of Thomas taking an egg right on the forehead—an image Thomas himself later said would probably be the one he was best known by.

Actually, Thomas got away relatively unscathed. With the mayor making speeches virtually every day about the Red Peril trying to infiltrate Jersey City, bands of civilians decided to supplement the nightstick with the fist and the boot. Late in May, two congressmen announced they would show their outrage over the Thomas kidnapping by making their own speeches in Journal Square. Several reporters turned up that night to watch the action. Journalists and Thomas supporters were lost in the vast crowd that filled the square: Legionnaires in full uniform marched around the square, blasting out music, ready to drown out any talk of constitutional rights; spectators surged back and forth as word went out that the congressmen had arrived. "At 10:45 the word came, 'They've called off the trip,' " one journalist recalled. "We told the news to Chief of Police Harry Walsh. 'It's just as well they didn't come,' he commented. 'It would have been murder if they had.' " After a drink, six reporters headed into the tube station for the ride home:

> From the top of the stairs, the screaming came. We ran up the stairs. A slugger gang was at work. Eight or ten of them, hard, strong, some of them wearing sweaters of the Jersey City Athletic League. They were thumping a little fellow, obviously a Jew. The Jew was sobbing, "Please, please, I'm a sick man." But they kept on swinging, gouging. He broke away, rushed down a staircase to the platform. They followed at a run. "Catch that God-damned Jew," one yelled at me as he ran by.
>
> They caught him and knocked him down. They punched and they kicked him—in the eye, the mouth, the stomach, the groin. Blood streamed across the tube platform, dripped down the side. "Leave me alone," the little Jew begged. "I didn't do nothing." Two station guards stood by, did nothing.
>
> We reporters were sick, but what could we do? Cowards, of course, all of us.

The unbridled thuggery in Jersey City was developing into a national scandal, but meanwhile Hague was facing a bigger problem. The CIO, backed up by the American Civil Liberties Union, was taking its challenge all the way to the U.S. Supreme Court. The justices delivered their opinion in 1939, and *Frank Hague et al. v. Congress of Industrial Organizations et al.* became a major defeat for Duh Mare. With all his ordinances barring public organizing struck down by the Court—which delivered a thorough scolding for good measure—Hague called off his dogs, and the CIO was allowed to work in peace.

The coda to the Skyway labor war came later in the decade, when Wisconsin senator Robert La Follette Jr. presided over a series of wide-ranging hearings between 1936 and 1941 on the ways the civil rights of labor unions and their members had been trampled by employers. On March 3, 1937, the La Follette Civil Liberties Committee—officially called the Senate Subcommittee Investigating Violations of Free Speech and the Rights of Labor—swore in Curtis S. Garner, general manager of erection for the American Bridge Company, to talk about the face-off between Teddy Brandle's ironworkers and the bridge companies.

The grim irony of the Skyway war was that not long after the twenty-one union members walked free, the steel industry bowed to the inevitable and recognized the AFL. That didn't do much for Edward Bergin, who appeared before the committee to explain that while he'd regained some limited use of his legs, his health remained poor and his settlement with American Bridge had netted him only four thousand dollars. When the committee members asked Garner if he felt the firm bore any moral responsibility for Bergin's shooting, Garner's answer was a definite no.

The senators then merrily grilled Garner over the reason why American Bridge had kept Bergin's assailant, Ralph

Golden, on the payroll until his subsequent trial and acquittal, Garner offered that the company had wanted to help the man out during a difficult period. La Follette also noted that the evidence file included numerous memos from Garner in which he fretted about the cost of keeping Jersey City police supplied with sandwiches and near beer as they helped guard the work site during the broiling summer months:

SENATOR LA FOLLETTE: The record shows, Mr. Garner, that you were very active and very alert to try to cut down the costs, or the extra costs, of this job, this open-shop job in New Jersey, including your desire to cut off the beer and the lunches, and so on. It amounted, however, to a substantial sum, did it not?

MR. GARNER: It did, Mr. Chairman.

SENATOR LA FOLLETTE: The amount on the ledger sheets, captioned "Labor trouble," introduced earlier, shows a total of $289,462.68. Do you recall the value of the contract?

MR. GARNER: That is a matter of record. I don't know whether I have it here or not.

SENATOR LA FOLLETTE: Was it $2,250,000?

MR. GARNER: It was over $2,000,000, Mr. Chairman.

SENATOR LA FOLLETTE: What would be your estimate of the additional expense your company would have borne had it met the union's demand and paid skilled workers an additional 25 cents an hour on this job?

MR. GARNER: That is a big order, Mr. Chairman. It is difficult to answer that. If you will allow me to tell you a little something about the conditions that existed there, I do not believe you would expect me to answer that, because no one knew what it would cost us to operate there. First of all—may I finish?

SENATOR LA FOLLETTE: I will confine my question, first, to what would have been the extra expense for labor on this job if you had paid $2 an hour for skilled workers instead of $1.75.

MR. GARNER: Well, that is over 10 percent in additional cost of labor.

SENATOR LA FOLLETTE: The total skilled man-hours on this job, as furnished by the company, was 207,396; and at an additional cost of 25 cents an hour, that would have amounted to $51,819 would it not?

MR. GARNER: I have not multiplied it out. Yes; it would.

SENATOR LA FOLLETTE: Whereas the total amount of additional expenses, as shown on the ledger sheets, was $289,462.68. Is that correct?

MR. GARNER: That is approximately correct.

In order to save itself twenty-five cents an hour on each salary, which would have cost another $51,819, the American Bridge Company had spent $289,462.68—over five times the cost it would have incurred by paying trained workmen an extra two dollars a day for performing dangerous work under demanding, dangerous conditions.

The firms that made up the National Erectors' Association couched their open-shop policy in terms like "the American Plan," and extolled the higher morality of not bargaining with unions. Luke Grant, who had already analyzed the conflicts between ironworkers and the NEA for the U.S. Commission on Industrial Relations, dismissed the NEA's arguments as "meaningless twaddle" in a 1919 report. "No matter how many high-sounding phrases may be used in discussing the subject," Grant wrote, "in the last analysis it is a common, ordinary question of dollars and cents."

The dread of paying an additional twenty-five cents per hour so obsessed the contractors on the Meadowlands viaduct that they used security guards who responded to rock-throwing men by using handguns.

The Skyway labor war is where rice pudding becomes blood pudding. Examining the record of the conflict with Ironworkers Local 45, it appears that men fought, maimed each other, and died—all for peanuts.

CHAPTER 9

Death Avenue

Perhaps it is time to say a good word for the poor, not so old Pulaski Skyway. That costly viaduct which shoots automobiles to and from the Holland Tunnel has come in for much unfavorable publicity as a death trap and playground for speed demons. But it is saving a lot of time for motorists, both those who know where they are going and those who don't. That's something in this speed-crazy age.

—*Newark Evening News*, editorial, December 13, 1933

Motorists who wish to test their skill on a modern highway should follow U.S. 1. . . . [F]rom Jersey City the road sweeps upward to Pulaski Skyway, giving a panorama of the New York hinterland, a region of smokestacks and marshes, of a few skyscrapers and many tenements, of patterns in steel rails and confusion in garbage dumps.

—Federal Writers Project, *New Jersey:
A Guide to Its Present and Past* (1939)

On the evening of October 11, 1933, a fleet of 150 black limousines set off from Newark Airport, lining up behind a rumbling phalanx of police cars. The limousines and their passengers—mayors, state and federal legislators, diplomats, a governor, and several military officers, along with their aides—headed east up Route 1 and climbed the steep access ramp leading to the Meadowlands viaduct and the span across the Passaic River.

When the motorcade reached the western end of the Passaic River span, Meyer Ellenstein, Newark's first Jewish mayor, pulled down a curtain that had been covering the letters of a sign that read GEN. PULASKI SKYWAY. The dignitaries paused for photographs, then continued along the Skyway's curved path to the eastern end of the Hackensack River span, where a similar sign was unveiled, this time by Mayor Frank Hague. A third plaque—a bas-relief portrait of General Pulaski created by John Skiba, a sculptor from nearby Irvington—was unveiled on the Jersey City approach to the Skyway by A. Harry Moore, governor of New Jersey and one of a long line of senators, representatives, governors, and judges personally selected and approved by Hague.

The motorcade then joined the crowd on Hudson Boulevard. Light, color, and music filled the air as the marchers— four thousand in all, according to the local papers—proceeded along the boulevard, past Journal Square and the business heart of Jersey City, headed west to pause at the entrance to Lincoln Park. In a city almost devoid of recreational space, Lincoln Park offered acres of ball fields and decorative ponds. On this night, it was a stadium, chosen because the playing fields on the western end afforded a view of the Skyway as it crossed the meandering flow of the Hackensack River. An estimated twenty thousand spectators jammed the floodlit park as Moore, Hague, and other honored guests took their places in the reviewing stand and watched the show.

And what a show. The Eighteenth Infantry Band, straight

This plaque bearing the image of
General Casimir Pulaski was placed on the Skyway
during the October 1933 dedication ceremony.

from Governors Island, led the procession, followed by several
regiments of the National Guard and their marching bands.
Veterans groups and Polish civic groups, all with their own
marching bands, came in behind, making the air shake with
the sound of drums and brass instruments. Genia Zielinska, a
member of the Chicago Opera, sang "The Star-Spangled Banner" and "Jeszscze Polska nie zginele," the Polish national an-
them. Her high, clear voice cut through the fall air, carrying
words of defiance from a European nation that had been raked
over many times by foreign armies, to an American city that
had long ago been conquered by the railroads.

Brigadier General Lucius Holbrook had been sent by the secretary of war himself to show Hague's pull with the federal government. In the crowd were scores of city workers and their families, all dependent on the Hudson County Democratic machine's largesse, all anxious to be seen showing up for the Boss.

Then there were speeches. The etiquette of politics requires that any decision or piece of legislation be hailed as an idea worthy of Einstein and an innovation worthy of Edison, so the legislators who put forth the idea of renaming the bridge—State Senator Edward P. Stout and Assemblyman Eugene W. Hejke—came in for large shares of praise. A fair number of Hudson County residents were of Polish descent. For them, Poland's struggle to maintain its independence and identity in the aftermath of the Great War was a source of ethnic pride. For politicians, that ethnic pride was reason enough to please a large and influential voting bloc.

Though the main newspaper, the *Jersey Journal,* covered the event, it refrained from directly quoting Hague's speech. This was a touchy point with the mayor. The sixth-grade dropout had never lost his second-generation Irish accent, and critics often mocked his tortured grammar. When angry or asserting his authority, the mayor was brutal and direct, delivering his lines in a deep, flat tone while thrusting his lower jaw forward—one chronicler of the period called it "Hague's dachshund-faced style of public speaking." When aiming for lofty public sentiments, however, Hague became lost in his own words; his speeches dissolved in a fog of abstractions and unfinished sentences. During one legendary radio address, Hague closed by saying, "Thank you, ladies and gentlemen, for the privilege of listening to me." Only the out-of-town papers liked to quote Hague, and when they did so it was usually not to his advantage.

So it fell to Governor A. Harry Moore, a natural speaker who could talk rings around friend and foe alike, and Holbrook to convey the proper martial spirit of the evening. They spoke of how Casimir Pulaski had seen his Polish homeland carved up by Prussia, Russia, and the Austrian Empire. After meeting Benjamin Franklin in Paris, Pulaski went to America in 1777 to throw in his lot with the patriots during the Revolutionary War, winning his spurs at the Battle of Brandywine, where he uttered his most famous line: "General Washington has gone to meet the enemy, and I go, too." He died in October 1779 of a wound sustained in the siege of Savannah.

"Today, we are going to meet the enemy and the enemy is the present depression," Moore said. "As our president, Franklin D. Roosevelt, goes forward to meet the enemy, let us, like Count Pulaski, say 'We go, too.' " Moore's words, delivered in his usual orotund, theatrical style, deliberately echoed Roosevelt's inaugural address and its charge that "the only thing we have to fear is fear itself—nameless, unreasoning, unjustified terror which paralyzes needed efforts to convert retreat into advance."

Actually, any driver who crossed the freshly christened Pulaski Skyway without the benefit of a police escort could have told Moore that there was plenty to fear besides fear itself.

For example, there was the prospect of driving across the Pulaski Skyway. Four days after the grand Pulaski dedication, a Hoboken policeman died in a collision while pursuing a speeding driver. Already, the Skyway's position as an automotive no-man's-land was being secured.

. . .

Within weeks of its original Thanksgiving Day opening in 1932, the Skyway revealed itself as a new kind of road in more ways than one. It was indeed a time-saving boon to drivers, but it was also a uniquely efficient generator of traffic accidents.

In a land where clogged streets and barely functional dirt roads were still the norm, the Skyway was an invitation to drivers to open up their engines. Imagine a driver emerging from the Holland Tunnel, then jockeying for position in traffic only to enter another tunnel—the depressed roadway beneath State Highway—and finally emerging onto the Skyway. The broad white lanes of concrete pavement, the majestic causeway curving across the wide-open landscape—what motorist could resist the opportunity to lead-foot it a bit?

Those who succumbed to the temptation, however, learned that the concrete pavement could be very slippery when wet. The roadbed, only fifty feet wide, had no shoulders but an ill-defined "breakdown lane" in the center that drivers regularly crossed, risking and often creating head-on collisions with oncoming vehicles. The crowning touch was the fact that access and egress ramps along the way were set like kiosks in the middle of the roadbed. Cars and trucks wheezing up the steep access ramps had to merge with the fastest-moving vehicles; drivers who miscalculated would inevitably swerve into the oncoming lanes to avoid a rear-end collision.

The Skyway's steep inclines and descents made it seem the most dangerous stretch of Route 25, but a state Motor Vehicles Commission survey released in October 1933—a mere five days after the Skyway was named in honor of the Polish war hero—found that the entire highway was the scene of forty-six traffic fatalities in the first nine months of the year. The Skyway alone had accounted for eight of those deaths. (By the end of the year, the total had reached sixty fatalities.)

The *Jersey Journal* editorialist cited two causes: "the callous disregard of many truck drivers for the rules and rights of the road, and the propensity of some auto drivers to hog the roadway by getting halfway between the fast and slow lanes while discussing blondes or the stock market or the menace of Hitler to world peace." The editorial closed with an admonishment:

All drivers using this magnificent skyway and highway should make up their minds to follow the Golden Rule. Those who want to move along should go into the fast lane and stay there; trucks and small-cars should get into the slow lane and stay there.

Those who want to weave should try the auto chute-the-chutes that may be found here and there along the road and which can be used for a small fee.

Barely two months after the Skyway was rededicated in Pulaski's honor, the *Newark Evening News* ran an editorial titled "The Bloodied Skyway" that assessed how badly things had gone wrong:

Designed as the last word in the safe expedition of traffic, the skyway has become the bloodiest section of highway in the state. The very assurance that everything has been done to prevent accidents seems to challenge some automobilists to prove the contrary. No cross-roads, no blind curves, no difficult grades and a superb road bed—and an accident record to make Death avenue in New York relinquish its title.

The editorial contradicted its own claims of "no difficult grades" by acknowledging that the Skyway posed a particular

Cars bound for Jersey City and the Holland Tunnel cross the Pulaski Skyway shortly after its opening. Note the absence of shoulders and the "suicide lane" in the center that was meant for disabled vehicles.

challenge to heavy trucks "occupying more than a lane of roadway, creeping up grades no faster than a walk and rolling down with irresistible momentum—these should be relegated to the parallel highway below."

Hague, who had taken to calling the Skyway a death trap, quickly heeded the call to ban trucks from the viaduct. A September 1933 study by the federal Bureau of Public Roads (which would later morph into the Federal Highway Administration) had shown that the Skyway attracted additional traffic by virtue of its convenience—drivers who had once avoided the route were now drawn to it. Also, the presence of the Kearny access ramp had indeed encouraged development, and dockside facilities had been developed along the Passaic River. More trucks were chugging slowly up the steep ramp and lumbering into the hurtling lines of cars. Though the viaduct was still vastly more convenient than the Meadowlands roads it had supplanted, the passage from the Holland Tunnel to Newark Airport could take as long as forty-five minutes when traffic was heavy. The Pulaski Skyway had generated as many problems as it has solved—the recurring theme of the automobile age.

By January 1934, Hague had won state approval for an ordinance banning trucks from the viaduct. Instead, the heavy traffic would be routed along nearby Communipaw Avenue, which was designated Truck Route 1-9. Trucking and haulers associations, not surprisingly, fought the ban in court. The effort was doomed, and by the end of the year the ban was fully in place. Once again, trucks bound to and from the Holland Tunnel were forced to negotiate the twists and turns of local streets in Kearny and Jersey City. In less than two years, the Skyway had become obsolete for much of its specific purpose.

In the mid-1940s, back home in Scarsdale, Fred Lavis looked back on the viaduct project as he wrote his memoirs.

Everybody was agreed on this design for the last link in the highway, when Sloan and I left the job at about the same time, he to England for the Foundation Company and I to take over the direction of the affairs of the International Railways of Central America. At the time we left, the plans for the reinforced concrete viaduct and the bridges were well along to completion but as soon as our backs were turned the vultures swooped, the advocates of unobstructed navigation took up the fight again and there was no one to say them nay. The result was the "Pulaski Skyway," an ungainly and unlovely structure of steel and the admiration of the crowd [sic] as a great example of engineering skill but so impractical in operation that trucks are not allowed to use it and its use for military purposes is greatly reduced.

Lavis was quick to add that he felt the engineers had done "a splendid job in meeting the conditions imposed on them, but in my estimation these conditions should never have been imposed." The revised design demanded by the Board of Commerce and Navigation, Lavis said, "adversely affects very large interests of the Public, public business and the commerce which have to cross these rivers. It benefits hardly at all the very small interests which the rivers serve or seem likely to serve in the future."

Lavis was correct to complain about the raising of the spans: for rivers that accommodated mostly barges, tugboats, and private craft, it was ridiculous to demand clearance of 135 feet. But there were flaws in Lavis's design that he could not recognize—flaws created by the novelty of his task—that would have been a problem no matter what, though the last-minute tampering certainly made them worse. The Wellington doctrine was fine for railroads, but the narrow roadbed and the use of left-lane access points—neither a problem for train traffic—proved disastrous for automobiles.

The same flaws could be seen at work across the Hudson River, where work on the West Side Highway (aka the Miller Elevated Highway) began in 1927 and wrapped up in 1931 as an elevated highway from West Seventy-second Street south to Chambers Street. The route was built as a replacement for Eleventh Avenue, which paralleled the New York Central Railroad's West Side Line. There were several grade crossings for cars and trucks trying to reach the ferries and docks, and there were so many horrific collisions between vehicles and trains that the street had been nicknamed "Death Avenue."

Its replacement, however, generated its own problems: like the Skyway, the West Side Highway had steep, narrow access ramps that were hard for trucks to negotiate, as well as left-lane access that might have been designed to set the stage for multiple collisions. If these turned out to be less lethal than crackups on Death Avenue or the Pulaski Skyway, it was only because the route's narrow roadbed and abrupt curves caused so many traffic tie-ups that drivers seldom built up enough speed for a fatal crash. In addition, the roadway was poorly drained, so that during heavy rainstorms drivers would find themselves up to their hubcaps in water, fifty feet above the ground.

Though the road is sometimes identified with the legendary builder and power broker Robert Moses, the elevated highway was already under way when Moses arrived on the scene. However, he did design the Henry Hudson Parkway to merge with it from the north, and he extended it to provide access to the Brooklyn–Battery Tunnel after a fight with preservationists— along with the timely intervention of Franklin Delano Roosevelt and the U.S. Navy—prevented Moses from realizing his dream of a Brooklyn–Battery suspension bridge that would have obliterated most of lower Manhattan.

The elevated road remained in use, inadequate and obsolete, until December 15, 1973, when the northbound lanes between Little West Twelfth and Gansevoort streets collapsed under the weight of a dump truck carrying some thirty tons of asphalt. The truck driver escaped serious injury, as did a tailgating motorist whose car tipped forward into the yawning hole in the roadbed, and the highway was immediately closed off. Over the next two decades, the highway was dismantled section by section, and until 1989 portions of it served as an unlikely sky-park for skaters and joggers.

In his book *Success Through Failure*, engineering writer Henry Petroski notes that advances in bridge building and other areas of design are frequently spurred more by failures than successes. The world applauded when Leon Moisseiff's design for the Golden Gate Bridge was realized in 1937. But it was the collapse of Moisseiff's even more elegantly designed Tacoma Narrows Bridge, which twisted apart and crashed into Puget Sound under high winds in 1940, that taught bridge builders how far they could go in reducing the weight (and construction costs) of their spans. The collapse of the bridge was filmed, and the footage is still shown to engineering students as a warning against architectural hubris.

The Pulaski Skyway should also be a part of those classes, if only as an example of a quieter kind of failure—a failure rooted not in recklessness, but in lack of background knowledge. The designers of Route 25 and the Skyway that is its most visible section were visionaries doing something that hadn't been done before. They weren't the only ones thinking in terms of superhighways—the first German autobahn was completed the same year the Skyway opened—but they were under the gun, and they had little experience in the field of traffic engineering to draw upon. The result was one of the most visually spectacular and functionally impaired mistakes ever made.

Unlike the West Side Highway, the Pulaski Skyway is too sturdy to collapse and too crucial to the New York metropolitan transit network to be closed down. Now and then some improvements are made: in the 1950s, the state installed an aluminum "Jersey barrier" to prevent head-on collisions, and covered the concrete deck with a less slippery surface. Work began in 2006 on a massive repaving project that will take years to complete. But there is really nothing more to be done with it. The Skyway will easily stand for another eighty years—a highway of the future that was instantly transformed into an antique.

CHAPTER 10

Steel and Ghosts

There is great affection and there is great history and there is great drama affiliated with [the Pulaski Skyway]. But now it's a royal pain.

—Tom Hart, Jersey City official, 1993

It's probably the most dangerous highway ever built, because you enter and exit on the fast lane. It's a great straightaway. There's no place for police to hide, and so everyone's just taking off.

—Russ Orrico, Jersey City police officer

The battle with the CIO was costly for Hague in ways that went beyond the Supreme Court decision. Though political insiders had long known of Hague's influence, the publicity surrounding the case and the thuggery deployed against Norman Thomas and others put Hagueville in the national spotlight. Frank Hague was about to become a household name, and an irresistible target.

The first two attacks came in quick succession early in 1938. The *New Yorker* subjected Hague to a withering profile, "Evolution of a Problem Child," and this was followed by an eight-page photo-essay in *Life*. Two years later, more trouble arrived in the form of Dayton David McKean's *The Boss: The Hague Machine in Action*, a book-length accumulation of evidence against Hague and every aspect of his career, written in the style of an outraged prosecutor. This was followed by a broadly insulting attack from the *Saturday Evening Post* in October 1940. The writer, Jack Alexander, called Hague "a mugg" and compared him to "some European dictators" in his control of the population:

> A heavy cloud of espionage hangs over the town. Policemen stop automobiles which they consider suspicious looking, force the occupants to get out and then search under mats and in luggage compartments. A driver with New York license plates may be forced to go to a station house and prove, through some Jersey City friend, that he has legitimate business in town. Plainclothesmen hang around gathering places like busy newsstands and restaurants and keep their ears cocked for some belittling reference to the mayor. One hears stories about cops breaking into homes without search warrants, but it is impossible to check the reports, as the people are afraid to talk. The cops are everywhere and citizens are afraid to discuss the mayor or his administration, except in whispers. Many Jersey Cityans will not talk politics over the telephone, for fear that their wires are being tapped.

But it was the *Life* essay that must have hurt the most. There's no telling how much smoke blowing Henry Luce's reporters engaged in to win the cooperation of Hague's people, but it's clear from some of the photographs that Duh Mare expected a flattering piece. What he got instead was a muckraking portrait so devastating that he immediately ordered all copies of *Life* removed from every newsstand in the city, with the threat of fines, increased taxes, and police harassment for any merchant foolish enough to flout the command. Like William M. Tweed, the legendary boss of old Tammany Hall who railed against "them damn pictures" drawn by Thomas Nast, Hague found himself under attack through a medium accessible even to the least-educated members of his working-class constituency.

The essay opens with a full-page portrait of Hague in one of his most commanding poses, buttoned up in one of the tight suits that showed off his still-muscular physique. On the opposite page, ranks of Jersey City's finest stand with nightsticks extended, as though waiting for directions on which heads to bust. There are images of city residents grimly lined up to pay their taxes, a glimpse of the New York skyline beneath a massive railway tank car, a family whose kitchen has become a miniature sweatshop, and, most woundingly, a panoramic shot of Hague's beloved medical center with a squalid, trash-strewn lot in the foreground.

One of the most striking images is placed near the end. Hague's attacks on the CIO and labor in general were loaded with denunciations of "Reds" and "Communists." On January 6, 1938, Hague summoned fifteen thousand residents to the city armory for a night of patriotic speeches and antilabor harangues. The image shows endless rows of chairs filled with dutiful listeners, all togged out in their finest clothes, while banners dangle in the smoky air: TIME TO STRIKE AGAINST THE RED INVASION, JERSEY CITY ONE HUNDRED PERCENT AMERICAN. One banner in particular adds a homegrown note of menace: MAYOR HAGUE APPEALS TO YOU TO STAY, with the added warning, DON'T LEAVE—YOUR PRESENCE REGISTERS YOUR

AMERICANISM. To emphasize the point, a police officer patrols the aisle, ready to take note of any un-American types who might succumb to the urge to leave early.

Given the level of fear Hague inspired at that point—it would be over a decade before he faced his final challenge—it's a macabre image of total, arrogant political control. How many hours went by that night until those listeners felt they could go home?

It would take nearly a quarter century for the state to deal with the endless logjam of truck traffic clogging the twists and turns of Route 1-9—traffic the Pulaski Skyway had been built to handle. When the solution arrived, it came almost as an afterthought, and under conditions that oddly mirrored those that had spurred construction of the Skyway and the Route 1 Extension.

Like the Route 1 Extension—though on a hugely greater scale—the New Jersey Turnpike was conceived hastily and built hurriedly. Just as the Route 1 Extension was the response to a project bringing in traffic from outside the state—the Holland Tunnel—so was the Turnpike a response to the construction of the imposing Delaware Memorial Bridge, which began in June 1948.

Navigation interests had opposed a span across the mouth of the Delaware River for over a decade, but the explosive growth in automobile traffic following World War II overwhelmed the ferry service that had been running since 1926 between Pennsville, New Jersey, and New Castle, Delaware. The federal War Department and the navy, which had stoutly refused to allow a bridge, finally relented. The highway departments of New Jersey and Delaware authorized the construction in 1945, and Congress gave its approval the next summer. Othmar Ammann, the architect of the George Washington Bridge, was appointed to design the 3,650-foot span—the first item in a postwar résumé that would include the Walt Whitman Bridge between Camden and Philadelphia (1957), the Throgs Neck Bridge in New York (1961), and the Verrazano-Narrows Bridge linking Staten Island and Brooklyn in 1964. For the Delaware Bay span, Ammann designed a suspension bridge that would lift traffic 188 feet above the waterline to avoid interfering with ships.

The New Jersey Highway Department had been mulling the idea of a huge expressway, dubbed Route 100, that would run the length of the state from the Delaware Bay coastline to the George Washington Bridge. With the Delaware bridge project already rolling, New Jersey governor Alfred E. Driscoll pushed hard, and the New Jersey Turnpike Authority was organized in October 1948. The next two years were a whirlwind of planning, design, and construction, and on November 5, 1951, the first 53 miles of the Turnpike were opened for use. A little over two months later, the rest of the 118-mile expressway was ready to take drivers from the eastern shore of Delaware Bay to the cliffs overlooking the Hudson River, and the George Washington Bridge.

The impressive speed with which the project was brought to completion was due in part to executive determination. The chairman of the Turnpike Authority, Paul L. Troast, started work by hanging a sign on his office door that read THE TURNPIKE MUST BE DONE NOV. '51, and he meant it. But the work was eased tremendously by the fact that more than half of the Turnpike's length cut through undeveloped farmland.

The northern half of the expressway, however, had to cut through heavily populated and industrialized areas. As the Turnpike entered the Meadowlands, engineers had to decide if they wanted to elevate the Turnpike over the Pulaski Skyway, or try to build beneath it. They opted to keep their expressway, and their costs, low. This allows commuters to get a fleeting up-close glimpse of the McClintic-Marshall Company's handiwork.

The city of Elizabeth was particularly hard-hit: the planners were penned in by Newark Airport to the west and the waterfront industries of the Elizabeth Seaport to the east. Faced with the wrath of thirty-two different industries, some of which vowed to leave New Jersey entirely if they were forced to relocate, the Turnpike Authority opted to avoid the waterfront and raze some 450 homes in an impoverished section of the city (the area's residents worried that the Turnpike would only expand the blighted area, a fear borne out by time). Like Jersey City, Elizabeth is a city split by transportation lanes—in Elizabeth's case, the Turnpike and Route 1-9. The Turnpike has been Elizabeth's version of the Erie Cut.

Jersey City's turn would come a few years later.

Teddy Brandle remained in Jersey City, living in a house at 398 Bergen Avenue, which he had deeded to his wife to hold off any foreclosure attempts. In June 1936 he circulated a petition to have himself reinstated as head of Local 45, but he withdrew when it became clear he had little support. A year later, Brandle tried to launch his own organization, unaffiliated with either the AFL or the CIO, and then in July 1938 he tried to win leadership of a local within the Newark Salesmen's Union, but each time he was undone by memories of "Brandleism" and the Hague administration's demolition work on uncooperative union locals. His chief comfort during this period came from a lawsuit he filed against Hague in July 1936 to recover sixty thousand dollars paid to the mayor to settle his income tax problems in 1930. Hague eventually settled with Brandle for thirty thousand dollars.

The Labor National Bank tower changed hands a number of times and was severely damaged by fire in March 1950. A new owner set out to rehabilitate the building in 1983; a year later, the structure was added to the National Register of Historic Places. Because of security concerns following the September 2001 terrorist attacks, visitors to the building have to enter through a side doorway and a long, narrow corridor. Once inside, however, they can see the grand lobby with its marble and dark polished wood, then admire the stained-glass barrel ceiling of the bank.

Brandle died November 29, 1949, after languishing for nearly five months in the Jersey City Medical Center, the place where he began his losing fight with Hague, and within sight of the tower that had once been the centerpiece of his short-lived empire. He lived long enough to see the reign of his old nemesis toppled, and doubtless took pride in the fact that his son, John Brandle, had an administrative post in the new regime that ran Hague's operation out of town.

By the mid-1940s, after three decades of power in which he had fended off legislative investigations and frustrated presidents, Frank Hague found himself in a tight corner. There had been several bids to revamp New Jersey's antiquated state constitution, and each time Hague had been able to block them. He was finally outfoxed by Republican governor Alfred E. Driscoll, who managed to win approval for a new constitution that, among other things, reorganized the judiciary in ways Hague had not foreseen.

In truth, Hague's control over his fiefdom had been weakening for several years. The old man spent more and more time abroad or at his mansion in Key Biscayne, leaving day-to-day operations in Jersey City in the hands of his bagman, John "Needlenose" Malone, who had been with Hague since his scuffling days with the Red Tigers gang. The organization's decision making became sclerotic, and formerly loyal operatives became restive. The nature of the city was changing, too, especially after World War II ended. The returning veterans, fresh from whupping two dictators overseas, were disinclined to bend the knee to the homegrown variety; they were more apt to see the machine as an antique overdue for replacement.

The 1940s had brought a series of bloody political battles. FDR gulled the old man into backing Charles Edison, son of the legendary inventor, for the New Jersey governorship. With Roosevelt's covert encouragement, Edison immediately launched investigations into key Hudson County offices. He was stymied by Hague's vigorous counterattacks and Roosevelt's withdrawal of support, but the organization had sustained its first hard blows. Edison's successor, a wealthy businessman and former U.S. senator named Walter Edge, kept up the heat by appointing a state attorney general who seized control of the Hudson County prosecutor's office. Bookmakers and numbers runners were the first to catch hell, but the pain spread as Hague appointees found themselves under indictment. The final blow came in 1947 when Driscoll's maneuver broke Hague's control over judicial appointments, demolishing the wall that had rendered Duh Mare and his minions immune to prosecution. A storm was coming; perhaps its force would diminish if Hague left of his own accord.

There was no question of his son, Frank Hague Jr., taking the reins: Hague fils had neither the political savvy nor the stern moralism of Hague père, and he was such a hopeless law student that Governor Moore simply appointed him to the state Court of Errors and Appeals in 1939 without bothering too much about his inability to graduate from any of the law schools he'd attended. Instead, Hague chose his nephew, Frank Hague Eggers, to don the municipal purple, and he formally turned over the gavel during a special session of the city commission, held June 1947 in the auditorium of Dickinson High School. The session was actually a gala retirement party in which Duh Mare sat surrounded by floral tributes as a seemingly endless stream of well-wishers stood at the microphone to sing Hague's praises. When it finally ended, a reporter intercepted Hague on the way out the door and asked what he was planning to do in the immediate future. "Get plenty of rest," Hague said. "Go to bed early nights and duck newspapermen."

Ironically, Eggers was well liked and showed signs of being an able and effective leader, but the shadow of Duh Mare chilled his chances of staying in power. Short and tubby rather than tall and lean, with owlish spectacles and a ready smile, Eggers commanded none of the fear Hague had inspired, and loyalty to the old man was being transferred to John V. Kenny, a Hague minion who had served his time with the expectation of better things when the boss retired. He was also the son of Ned Kenny, the saloon owner whose cigar box full of cash provided the start for Hague's political career, and younger brother of Frank Kenny, whose murder had allowed Hague to showcase his determination to uphold law and order.

Hague himself did nothing to make it easier for Eggers. Even when staying in his Florida mansion, Hague kept in close contact via telephone. When it came time for Eggers to toss out the first ball at Roosevelt Stadium in 1948, Hague was photographed standing at his elbow, apparently talking shop with Needlenose Malone. Eggers looked like an eager little boy playing games while the grown-ups talked business. When

Harry S. Truman made the obligatory Hudson County pilgrimage during the 1948 presidential campaign, Eggers was
photographed shaking his hand while the old mayor loomed
behind them, the expression on his face registering either
great distaste (he and Truman detested each other) or unen-
durable fatigue.

Kenny led the "Freedom Ticket" bolstered by support from
labor unions and returned World War II veterans who saw
the Hague machine as the legacy of a corrupt, over-the-hill
dictator—they even adopted Winston Churchill's "V for Victory" gesture as their own. When Kenny's fusion ticket defeated Eggers in May 1949, a crowd swarmed in front of City
Hall, singing "Now Is the Hour" as they raised a coffin and a
sign saying "Here Lies the Remains of the Hague Machine,
36 Years of Age." (For all his public cockiness, Kenny was so
afraid of Hague that he had a car waiting to spirit him to
Newark Airport if the election went against him.) *Life* maga-
zine, which had helped expose Hague to national ridicule in
1938, sent photographers to cover the rout and published them
in a new photo-essay, triumphantly titled "Jersey City Throws
Out Boss Hague." A few months later, Governor Driscoll won a
second term, crushing Elmer H. Wene, Hague's handpicked
gubernatorial candidate.

Though Kenny's administration would prove to be more
than equal to Hague's organization in venality, it was much in-
ferior in terms of effectiveness. Nevertheless, Kenny got considerable mileage from his victory, and he continued to attack
Hague whenever possible. When Eggers died of a stroke in
1954, Hague cut short a trip to Paris to attend the funeral.
Kenny arranged for a process server, Leo Gatoni, to present
Hague with a subpoena in front of the funeral home. Still a
brawler at seventy-eight, Hague clenched his fists to slug the

man, but the funeral director stepped in and Hague allowed himself to be led into the funeral home, his face a mask of rage.

The Turnpike Authority started work on the Newark Bay–Hudson County Extension in 1953. The path of the offshoot expressway would snake its way east from Elizabeth to cross the upper reaches of Newark Bay, then enter Jersey City as it curved along the southern extreme of Bergen Hill. Seen from a distance, the immense viaduct—opened to great fanfare in 1956—is a showcase for big engineering at its most imposing, crossing the landscape on tall concrete piers, casting a shadow on neighborhoods and local streets as it curves to join with traffic emerging from the depressed roadway that serves as the gateway to the Skyway.

That same year, a bedridden President Dwight D. Eisenhower signed into law the Federal-Aid Highway Act, which started the decades-long task of creating America's own version of the autobahn system, on a vastly greater scale. Eisenhower had started the ball rolling with his highway "Grand Plan" in 1954, but his advocacy of a national highway system was rooted in his three-month trek with the army's convoy along the Lincoln Highway in 1919, and reinforced by his appreciation of the German autobahn network, which he saw firsthand during World War II. "The old convoy had started me thinking about good, two lane highways, but Germany had made me see the wisdom of broader ribbons across the land," he later wrote.

The New Jersey Turnpike extension was an extremely mixed blessing for Jersey City. It removed much of the slow-moving truck traffic from Route 1-9 and gave it a clear path to the Holland Tunnel—the very purpose the Pulaski Skyway had been intended to serve decades earlier. But it created another corridor of blight through a city already chopped up by highways and rail lines. It also showed up the curious contrast between the up-to-the-minute improvements dedicated to channeling traffic through Jersey City, and the antiquated maze of local roads that made traveling within the city such a headache.

Former state assemblyman Alan Karcher, whose pastime was the study of how the residue of old political battles continues to taint the present, has suggested that a big part of the problem lay with Mayor John V. Kenny and his resistance to improvements for the city's streets, even the baffling maze that the Tonnele Circle had become:

> Kenny always emphasized that any such widenings or upgradings would only take business away from the Turnpike. I was puzzled as to why Mayor Kenny would be so solicitous of the Turnpike's revenue stream. My initial thought was that he wanted to make sure it was making enough money to keep his army of payroll patriots employed. Only when I was much older and wiser did I find out that his concern for the Turnpike's fiscal soundness emanated from his having millions of dollars in unregistered Turnpike bearer bonds.

La plus ça change, plus c'est la même chose. Frank Hague might not have been able to read that saying in the original French, or even pronounce it correctly, but he probably would have appreciated the underlying sentiment: *The more things change, the more they stay the same.*

•   •   •

The ironworkers caught up in the Skyway labor war returned to their old lives and their old jobs. Many of them stayed in Hudson County, or moved to new homes not very far away. In many cases, their children and grandchildren became ironworkers themselves. For them, the War of the Meadows is a dimly recalled family legend. Jim Bergin, still living in northern New Jersey, remembers his grandfather Edward as a man who needed crutches and braces to move, and couldn't even go to the toilet without help. He grew up hearing stories that his grandfather had been shot and partially paralyzed, but spent most of his life unaware of the circumstances under which it happened.

"Star" Campbell, the man who had endured so much of Hague's wrath, returned to the headlines a couple of times as a supporter of Brandle's comeback efforts. Before long, though, he too faded back into the background life of the city. John Drewen, the prosecutor who had done his level best to send Campbell to death row, was duly elevated to a judicial post a few years after the Skyway case ended. The murder trial that had roiled Jersey City sank beneath the surface and was covered over by the daily flow of events and the enormous changes wrought by the Depression, Roosevelt's election, and eventually the anxieties of World War II.

Hague spent his last years in a luxurious Park Avenue apartment, a few miles, several million dollars, and a wide, deep river away from his Horseshoe birthplace. The man who had once declared he would live and die in the Horseshoe now avoided Jersey City and his old Hudson County stomping grounds. The incident at the funeral home would not be repeated.

They were busy years, full of trips to Europe and cruises with his wife of fifty years, the former Jenny Warner. But they were also gloomy years, haunted by old regrets. As Thomas Fleming recalled:

There's a wonderful anecdote that [Frank Hague's] daughter told me. When [Hague] was out of power and out of politics, living over in New York, he had trouble sleeping. He'd wake up in the middle of the night and he'd start thinking of how things had gone over the years, and he'd remember some family that he had ruined. Whether he'd driven the guy out of Jersey City or he'd ruined his law practice because he'd come out against him, or fired him off the cops because he'd talked too much in a bar against Hague, that sort of thing. And he would get the person's phone number and he'd call them up in the middle of the night, and he'd say, "You know, I was thinking of the old days, and I was a good friend . . ." Maybe he'd get the daughter, or the son, something like that, very often the guy would be dead by then. And he'd say, "You know, I was thinking of the old days, and I was a good friend of your father before we had that falling out. Is there anything I can do for you?" And now this— you've gotta be Irish to understand this—every single one of them said, "No, we don't want anything from *you.*" As somebody said, the definition of Irish Alzheimer's is: You forget everything but your grudges.

Hague died of complications from bronchitis and asthma on New Year's Day, 1956, about two weeks before his eightieth birthday. Hudson County legend has it that his last words were

"I never thought you two bastards would outlive Frank Hague," spoken to Needlenose Malone and John Milton, the attorney who had faithfully supervised Hague's all-cash business dealings.

His funeral drew huge crowds. "Frank Hague has come home to Jersey City for the last time," a *Jersey Journal* editorialist wrote, and he was eulogized in the national press as the last of the old-time political bosses—a description that would be reused many more times in years to come.

Hague's resting place is one of the grandest tombs in Holy Name Cemetery, one of Jersey City's most opulent Catholic cemeteries. The far grander Jersey City Medical Center, which Hague considered the cornerstone of his legacy, remained a fiscal white elephant and gradually declined under successive administrations. The maternity hospital closed in 1979, and the other buildings in the complex emptied out over the years. By the end of the twentieth century, most of the buildings brooding on the crest of Bergen Hill had been abandoned, many of them stripped of plumbing and wiring by scavengers, and the Jersey City Medical Center was reconstituted into a two-building complex in 2004.

The vacant remnants of the medical center were purchased in 2005 by a developer, Metrovest Equities of New York, with an eye to converting the ten high-rise buildings into luxury residential space encompassing 1,100 individual condo and apartment units, along with restaurant and theater space. As of late 2006, conversion work was under way on the first two buildings of the complex, which the developer had renamed the Beacon. As part of the $350 million conversion plan (the largest approved by the state for a 20 percent federal tax credit under the Federal Historic Rehabilitation Tax Credit program), Hague's mahogany-paneled medical center office was to serve as a game room for poker players—perhaps not an inappropriate fate.

It was only to be expected that *Weird NJ*, a publication devoted to the Garden State's odder folkways and obscure haunts, would eventually find its way to the Pulaski Skyway. In issue 28, two correspondents describe hiking from the PATH station in Journal Square to the Broadway access ramp, then climbing to begin a hair-raising walk along the viaduct's narrow steel curb. "The views of the industrialized reaches of the Meadowlands and the New York skyline in the distance were majestic," the writer notes, "views glimpsed in the brief moments I could tear my eyes away from the vehicles bearing down on us."

The goal of their walk across the viaduct, which took about an hour, was the steel plaque with relief sculpture of General Pulaski. Goal attained, they continued toward Newark, scampering along the steel curb as cars roared past, mere inches from their bodies.

Actually, *Weird NJ* missed a trick—walking across the Skyway isn't weird, merely suicidal. True weirdness took place early in the afternoon of July 14, 1950, when a man leading a mule and a dog along the right lane brought westbound traffic to a halt on the Hackensack River span, causing a traffic jam that stretched all the way back to the Holland Tunnel. The man, fifty-eight-year-old Clarence Hornbeck of Galesburg, Illinois, told police his mule, Devil's Brother, had been upset by the honking, cursing motorists streaming past in the left lane and, when a pack slipped from his back, refused to go any farther.

Hornbeck, an apparition in a patched jacket and top hat, had bet a friend back in Galesburg that he could walk all the way to New York City and bum a cigarette off Arthur Godfrey, the affable radio and television personality. Hornbeck had indeed hoofed it all the way to Manhattan with only his dog, Smoky, and his mule for company. When he arrived in mid-June, the New York police stabled Devil's Brother along with their horses for the next few weeks. They also tried to help Hornbeck contact Godfrey. The celebrity host apparently didn't want to play along, and the disappointed Hornbeck was on his way back to Illinois when Devil's Brother had his little episode on the Pulaski Skyway.

Jersey City police rerouted Hornbeck to the alternate ground-level highway and got traffic across the Skyway moving again before the evening rush hour. When last seen, Hornbeck and his animals were trudging along Route 1, headed back to Galesburg and, presumably, a reckoning on the bet.

Jersey City was a different place—wearier, shabbier, more crime-ridden and down on its luck—when the Pulaski Skyway was rededicated in 1978 to mark the approach of its fiftieth anniversary. About two hundred dignitaries gathered for the Sunday afternoon ceremony on September 17. Instead of Lincoln Park, the Skyway itself was the stage for the ceremony, as the attendees trooped up the steep entry ramp at Kearny and sat on chairs set out on the roadbed.

Needless to say, hardly any of the participants in the first dedication were around for the rededication: Genia Zielinska once again sang "The Star-Spangled Banner" and "Jeszscze Polska nie zginele," albeit without the same force she mustered in 1933. The mayor presiding over the event was Thomas F. X. Smith, who was in many ways the physical opposite of Frank Hague: a gregarious glad-hander of average height, with a full head of curly back hair and a ready smile.

The songs and speeches filled the empty air within the

black girders. The Skyway had been closed to Sunday traffic at 1 p.m., and cars were lining up along the parallel Route 1 alternate path. No doubt the drivers could have supplemented the high-minded speeches with some observations of their own, but they were far away, and the speeches and singing would have drowned them out.

During the mid-1930s, the Works Progress Administration, or WPA, put some 8.5 million Americans to work on various repair and maintenance projects requiring manual labor. That workforce included about 6,500 musicians, painters, and writers whose talents were employed to chronicle daily life in a country just starting to get back on its feet. Part of that effort was the Federal Writers Project, which employed hundreds of writers—some of whom, such as Nelson Algren, Ralph Ellison, and Zora Neale Hurston, would go on to major literary careers—to prepare guidebooks to the states. Each book was built around "tours" that spotlighted points of interest along each route.

The Garden State edition—*New Jersey: A Guide to Its Present and Past,* republished in the 1990s under the title *The WPA Guide to 1930s New Jersey*—benefited from the contributions of such luminaries as Louis Adamic, Edmund Wilson, and William Carlos Williams. The first photograph featured in the book is the dome of the state house in Trenton, immediately followed by an aerial shot of the Pulaski Skyway, its concrete piers and road deck still unsullied by time, almost startlingly white in the sun.

The book opens with a tour that starts in Fort Lee, at the threshold of the George Washington Bridge, and follows Route 1 all the way to Trenton. Along the way, naturally, it describes what is to be seen of Jersey City and the Meadowlands:

The meadowlands have their own skyline. On the banks of the Hackensack River stand the six great chimneys of a Public Service Electric and Gas Co., and a gas and coke plant. Beyond are small hills of coke, several times the height of a freight car. The towers of railroad and highway drawbridges are close by.

From there, the tour joins the Pulaski Skyway, "a pioneer achievement in the solution of the problem of handling through traffic in one of the most congested traffic areas in the world":

No towering office buildings dominate Jersey City's skyline, but rather the broad bulk of the Old Gold cigaret and the Listerine factories and, dominating all, the light gray units of the American Can Co. plant, close to the highway. The gray stone clock tower of St. John's Catholic Church, near Journal Square in the heart of Jersey City, stands out.

The skyway rises to the cantilever span crossing the Hackensack River. Were it not for the heavy I-beam railing, there would be excellent views of the waterways adjacent to New York Harbor and of the Newark industrial area. Full views are possible only when the two high points of the skyway are crossed; from those points are seen the tall office buildings of Newark, almost hidden by the gas tanks of Harrison. To the [left], seen by a right-angle glance through the railing, is one of the great garbage dumps for which the Newark meadows are famous. Next is the large Western Electric Co. plant, at the head of Newark Bay where the Hackensack and Passaic Rivers unite. The sun glints sharply from the roofs of hundreds of employees' cars, parked in neat formation next to the factory. To the rear are the towers of midtown and then downtown Manhattan, then the slight elevation that is Brooklyn, the gap of the Narrows (entrance to New York Harbor) and finally the hilly outline of Staten Island, 8 miles south. The haze from factory smoke often obliterates part of the landscape, and the no-parking rule makes use of field glasses impracticable.

Today, much of the vista described by the WPA guide has been rendered invisible by the haze of air pollution: it's a rare, crisp day that one can see as far as Brooklyn, let alone Staten Island or the Narrows. The Pulaski Skyway has never been a place where it is advisable to stop and scan the landscape with binoculars, but it's even less so now.

As for the area below the Skyway, South Kearny has even more chain-link fencing and barbed wire now than it did when Brandle's men faced off against the Foster detective agency and the Jersey City police. The Kearny access ramp was included at Hague's insistence as a way to promote industrial development, and his vision has been realized in a suitably gritty way: this place is all business. Every road seems to dead-end at a fenced-off yard, and every building presents a blank front to the passerby, as if to say that if you don't already know what's going on inside, you don't need to know.

The most inviting-looking places here are Goldie's Kosher Truck Parts and the Skyway Diner, a trucker hangout dwarfed by the black girders above and the looming tractor-trailers all around. The interior is an oasis of turquoise Naugahyde seats; the walls are decorated with photographs commemorating the time a film crew shot a scene for *The Sopranos* in which a pair of gunsels try to assassinate a young mobster as he leaves the diner. Listen in on the conversations and one realizes that this particular section of the Skyway shelters a small community devoted to tending big trucks.

Back outside, there is the odd sensation of feeling completely isolated in a densely packed, thoroughly developed area. Nobody walks here. Nature has not so much been conquered as despoiled: everything except the river has been covered with asphalt, wire, or steel, and the river is practically simmering with pollutants.

Are there ghosts? Do the sounds of pitched battles between picketers and guards vibrate in the air—steel bolts rattling against concrete and metal, fists and clubs smacking into flesh? Do the looming concrete piers of the Skyway occasionally echo with the lost cries of workmen who paid the dreadful price for a moment's inattention?

If so, then they are drowned out—masked by traffic noise and the endless hum of cars, thousands of them, speeding invisibly overheard, bound for the Holland Tunnel, where the story of America's first superhighway began, and where this story now reaches its end.

Roads once connected communities; now they separate them. Roads used to bring welcome news and fresh information; now they bring noise and pollution. Roads were once a part of the landscape; now they shape the landscape. The Route 1 Extension was the harbinger of that change. Most of the route has been modified beyond recognition, but its most visible portion, the Pulaski Skyway, remains virtually unchanged three quarters of a century after it was welded into place. Anyone who wants to find the demarcation line between the time that roads served as a means to an end and our current predicament—in which roads are often an end in themselves—need only look here.

Reminders of that earlier era can still be found, many of them less than an hour's drive from the Skyway, in Colonial-vintage towns where stone houses nuzzle the shoulders of the road, or in rapidly suburbanizing farm communities where the fields now yield up town houses, McMansions, subdivisions, shopping malls, and corporate parks. Here, where secondary roads are swelling with highway-capacity traffic as the pressure of development increases, there are still farmhouses that were built to hug the road so the residents could know if the mail had come, or a friend was riding past, or somebody new was in town. They sit out of place between sprawling corporate campuses and strip malls, sometimes hidden behind hedges, with their windows curtained and their owners (assuming the house is still inhabited; many are long vacant) doing their best to ignore the traffic hurtling past within a few feet of their front doors.

Houses are now built as far from the road as possible. Highways are now a source of convenience and danger. The dawn of the superhighway age set the stage for phenomenal economic growth throughout America. It also helped foster the decline of the cities, as residents flocked to the suburbs metastasizing around urban boundaries; ushered in the use of highways as barriers against undesirable neighborhoods (as was done in Chicago during the reign of Mayor Richard Daley); or led to inadvertent creation of such neighborhoods, as when the opening of the Cross-Bronx Expressway in 1963 accelerated the decay of the South Bronx.

In the early years of the twenty-first century, as the suburbs in many areas have grown as dense and troubled as the cities their builders fled, it appears that the great mistake of the automobile age was to encourage the disposal of its predecessor, the railroad era, so quickly and thoroughly. The wonderful mobility and flexibility of driving one's own car blinded everyone to the fact that with more and more drivers getting in on the action, the fun would soon cease. The term "rush hour" is universally recognized as an ironic joke: when workplaces empty out and thousands of drivers take to the road, nobody can rush anywhere in the resulting gridlock. The disorderly patterns of development encouraged by the automobile make it difficult, even impossibly expensive, to expand mass transit with new rail lines. Even in areas where rights-of-way and train tracks remain in place, communities now press in close around existing tracks. Their residents fight to keep old train lines from being upgraded to passenger status, and who can blame them? Who wants high-speed passenger trains crashing past backyards and along grade crossings?

And yet the only alternative—more buses along already congested highways—simply intensifies traffic problems by creating traveling bottlenecks as buses plod from stop to stop. In the 1990s, New Jersey and California attempted to mold public habits and encourage carpooling by creating left-hand "diamond lanes" along major three-lane highways that could be used only by cars with more than one occupant. The experiment was a disaster. With work sites scattered across dozens of miles of roadway, carpooling was only a pipe dream. Single-driver cars remained the majority, only they were now crammed into two lanes of traffic, moving slowly, adding to pollution, creating traffic jams, and setting the stage for enraged confrontations as diamond-lane drivers, reaching their destinations, found their way blocked by resentful motorists in the other two lanes.

This is the world the engineers of the Route 1 Extension and the Pulaski Skyway were helping to create—little did they realize. By building a bridge to the future, they helped create a future. To chart a course into the unknown, they fell back on what they knew. Like all of us, they stood with one foot in the past as they tried to plan for something they could scarcely imagine: sprawl, congestion, a landscape ruled by automobiles.

Our plans and our actions are circumscribed by the decisions of dead men; our highways and bridges were charted and built by hands long since gone to dust. Ozymandias, speaking from his stone monument, challenged: *Look on my works, ye mighty, and despair!* His successors, speaking from monuments like the Pulaski Skyway, would have to use more modest phrasing: *It seemed like a good idea at the time.* Their real challenge, yet to be taken up, would be: *Could you have done any better? Can you now?*

That remains to be seen.

ACKNOWLEDGMENTS

The great engineer Othmar Ammann once said that anyone who would take exclusive credit for bridge design was an egotist. The same is true for a nonfiction book. Every page of this one benefited from the (sometimes inadvertent) advice and aid of someone else, and to all of them I offer thanks.

Thanks to the late Charles Cummings, a talking book of New Jersey history and an endlessly helpful man I would liked to have known better and longer.

Thanks to Rick C. Lavis, descendant of the engineer Fred Lavis, who opened his family records to me.

Thanks to Bob Leach, author of *The Frank Hague Picture Book* and numerous articles and essays about the Boss, who put me in touch with Esther Meers, former secretary to Teddy Brandle.

Thanks to the remarkable staffs at the Newark Public Library, the Jersey City Free Public Library, and the Secaucus Public Library. Thanks to the Alexander Library staff on the main campus of my alma mater, Rutgers University.

Thanks to the two unrelated Flemings who played a role in my research: Robert Fleming, an ironworker who gave me insights into the mind-set of men working on high steel, and acted as a liaison with colleagues descended from the men caught up in the Skyway labor war; and the distinguished historian and novelist Thomas Fleming, who connected me with Robert Fleming and whose fine memoir *Mysteries of My Father*, published while I was deep into researching the Hague administration, gave a fresh, personal angle on the subject.

Thanks to Dennis Murphy of the Hudson County courthouse, who spent a great deal of time trying to track down trial records from the Skyway murder case—an ultimately futile quest he undertook with great courtesy and interest.

Thanks to the Society for Commercial Archaeology.

Thanks to Leigh Davis for her computer expertise, enthusiastically offered and generously given.

Thanks to my editor, Diane Wachtell, whose suggestions and corrections steadied my hand as I chipped away to the shape within this particular stone.

Special thanks to my literary agent, Michele Rubin of Writers House, whose instincts about where to find a home for this story were dead-on accurate.

And above all, love and thanks to my family: Mary, my wife, and my daughters, Carolyn and Torgyn. Thanks for faith, encouragement, and patience with all the bizarre drawbacks of life with a writer: odd silences, weekends spent sequestered within the study, periodic stretches of oblivious musing, and bouts of Roderick Usher–level sensitivity to noises and distraction. At times like that, even I wouldn't put up with me, but—fortunately for me—you do.

NOTES

Introduction

1 *That was a terrible time* . . . Jim Bergin, telephone interview with the author, March 23, 2005.

6 *the Skyway conflict set the stage* . . . Karcher, *New Jersey's Multiple Municipal Madness*, p. 188.

1. The Three Barriers

11 *The first fifty-cent toll* . . . Details of the Holland Tunnel opening are from Mysak with Schiffer, *Perpetual Motion*, p. 78.

12 *Travelers from New York in the 1700s* . . . Sullivan, *The Meadowlands*, p. 107.

14 *Nothing has spread socialistic feeling* . . . Gerald Carson, "Goggles and Side Curtains," *American Heritage*, April 1967.

16 *In 1903, a Vermont physician named H. Nelson Jackson* . . . Hokanson, *The Lincoln Highway*, p. xvi.

19 *The U.S. Army got into the act* . . . See Pete Davies, *American Road*, for a highly readable account of this trek.

20 *The great engineer Gustav Lindenthal proposed* . . . Petroski, *Engineers of Dreams*, pp. 211–16.

23 *Visitors to the tunnels* . . . *The Eighth Wonder*, p. 47.

24 The fifty-foot geyser is reported in Ernest A. McKay's history of the Holland Tunnel, *Invention & Technology*, Fall 1988.

25 *Goethals favored a masonry tunnel design* . . . Petroski, *Engineers of Dreams*, p. 233.

25 *Owners of Jersey City properties that would be razed* ... Fleming, *Mysteries of My Father,* p. 156.

26 *On May 31, Holland slipped into the Erie rail yard* ... Petroski, *Engineers of Dreams,* p. 236.

26 *At one point, the New Jersey commissioners* ... *New York Times,* December 15, 1921.

26 *When Holland staged his clandestine groundbreaking* ... "Tunnel Ceremony Late but Not Off," *Newark Evening News,* June 27, 1922.

27 For more color on Boyle's role as attack dog for the Hague machine, see "Attempt to Seize Shoe Land to Be Fought in Court," *Jersey Journal,* April 27, 1922. See also "Hague Ultimatum to Tunnel Board," *Jersey Journal,* April 28, 1922.

2. The Horseshoe Against the World

31 *For those who don't remember him, Frank Hague* ... Thomas Fleming, "My Life as a Historian," *History News Network,* October 9, 2002, http://hnn.us/articles/1008.html.

31 *[Hague] was almost a demigod to the people* ... Leroy McWilliams, *Parish Priest,* 234–35.

36 For an account of the Black Tom explosion, see Marc Mappen, *Jerseyana,* p. 155.

38 *The Great McGinty,* a 1940 comedy written and directed by Preston Sturges, shows its hero getting started in politics by working as a floater.

38 *The Horseshoe was to Frank Hague* ... Dayton David McKean's *The Boss: The Hague Machine in Action* is, for all its obvious prejudices, the Ur-text of Frank Hague studies. McKean's account of Hague's early years (pages 28–45) is echoed through all subsequent profiles.

41 *Published as a slender book in 1905, Plunkitt's stories* ... Riordan, *Plunkitt of Tammany Hall.*

3. The Slanted Road

50 *Most of the 16,000-foot length of the viaduct* ... Condit, *American Building Art,* p. 110.

53 *If all goes well, the driver hits* . . . Details of the Skyway's sections are taken from Mary McCahon and Sandra G. Johnston's analysis, prepared for the National Register of Historic Places nomination.

57 Background information taken from Lavis's *Memoirs,* also his obituary in the *New York Times,* November 26, 1950.

58 *Everything about the man* . . . Bill Quirk, "Fred Lavis, Consulting Engineer, Cautions on Foreign Construction," *Contractors and Engineers Monthly,* March 1945.

59 *Shortly after we arrived* . . . Ibid.

60 The story of the assault on Mrs. Lavis comes from an undated newspaper clipping in the collection of Rick C. Lavis. The item, headlined "American's Duel with a Mexican," is bylined "Special Dispatch to the Globe-Democrat." The date is not available, but the story notes that the attack took place along the "Chihuahua and Pacific Railroad" construction route, which at least offers a time frame.

62 *He [Sloan] said it was a problem* . . . Lavis, *Memoirs,* p. 486.

63 *I didn't like the idea* . . . Lavis, *Memoirs,* p. 488.

64 *Lavis's partner on the project* . . . "S. Johannesson, 75, a Civil Engineer," *New York Times* obituary, February 23, 1953.

67 *Furthermore, Lavis noted in the 1927* . . . Lavis, "Economic Theory of Highway Location."

70 *We know that when the vehicular tunnel opens* . . . TAMS Study, 14.

72 The last-minute design changes to the Skyway are covered by McCahon and Johnston in "Sections Three Design Changes—the Pulaski Skyway Controversy," pp. 20–22, and by the TAMS study, "Pulaski Skyway Controversy and Resolution," pp. 22–28.

4. Rice Pudding

75 The Jersey City catechism is from Leroy McWilliams, *Parish Priest,* p. 234.

75 The terms "organization" and "rice pudding" are defined by Thomas Fleming in Goldensohn and Cohen, *The Life and Times of Frank Hague.*

77 The Alsop column appeared in the *New York Herald Tribune,* June 6, 1936.

77 *"Delivering" also applied* . . . Dayton David McKean, *The Boss,* p. 133.

78 *The people in Jersey City laughed at Tammany* . . . *The Life and Times of Frank Hague.*

78 *Under Hague, one observer recalled* . . . McWilliams, *Parish Priest,* pp. 74–75

79 See Nelson Johnson, *Boardwalk Empire,* pp. 98–102, for more on "Nucky" Johnson and the 1929 gangster convention in Atlantic City.

81 "Graft and Comedy Revealed in Jersey City," *New York Post,* November 3, 1928.

82 For an excellent summary of Hague's rise to statewide power, see Richard J. Connors's *A Cycle of Power,* which is second only to McKean's *The Boss* in the curriculum of Frank Hague studies.

86 The description of "skyscraper men" is from Adamic, *Dynamite,* p. 190.

86 The career of "walking delegate" Sam Parks is chronicled by Seidman, *Labor Czars,* pp. 18–26.

88 *"the amazing Teddy Brandle* . . ." Bernstein, *The Lean Years,* pp. 340–41.

88 *Brandle "no ordinary man,"* . . . Ibid., pp. 149–56.

89 *Hague and Brandle had a mutual acquaintance* . . . Katcher, *The Big Bankroll,* p. 275.

89 Brandle's card-index system is explained by reporter David Wittles, "The Hague Machine," *New York Post,* February 7, 1938.

89 *Brandle proved his worth to Hague* . . . McKean, *The Boss,* pp. 184–87.

91 Esther Meers spoke with the author in a telephone interview on August 30, 2004. She was ninety-three at the time.

94 *In the fall of 1931, a Newark contractor* . . . Wittles, "The Hague Machine."

5. Burned Bridges

97 *If a man says to me the McNamaras*... Adamic, *Dynamite,*
p. 198.

97 *The apple peddler*... Horan, *The Desperate Years,* p. 13.

102 *"one of the most determined and brutal*..." Adamic, *Dynamite,*
p. 191.

102 The "Dynamite Conspiracy" is well summarized in Rasenberger, *High Steel,* pp. 177–89.

104 *When this contract was let*... Garner's testimony comes from
the records of the U.S. Senate Subcommittee Investigating Violations of Free Speech and the Rights of Labor, exhibit 77,
2582.

6. The War of the Meadows

107 *What we are passing thru at Jersey City*... U.S. Senate Subcommittee Investigating Violations of Free Speech and the
Rights of Labor, exhibit 781, p. 2585.

112 Details of the ironworkers' trade can be found in Mitchell's
essay "The Mohawks in High Steel." Collected in *Up in the Old
Hotel.*

112 *Brandle's best shot at unionizing*... "Machine Gun in Labor
Auto, Brandle Told," *Jersey Journal,* July 9, 1931.

113 *There were also worrisome rumors*... *Jersey Journal,* July 15,
1931.

120 *"Police were ordered today*..." "5 Attacked, 1 Dying, as Brandle Men Riot," *Jersey Journal,* February 27, 1932.

120 "Open Shop Man Fatally Beaten," *Newark Evening News,* February 28, 1932.

121 *William "Star" Campbell slipped the belt off his raincoat*...
"Tries to End Life in Cell," *New York Times,* July 14, 1932.

7. High, Wide, and Handsome

124 *Late in the afternoon, Theodarokis*... "Painter Killed in Fall
from New Highway," *Newark Evening News,* October 15, 1932.

133 The opening of the Meadowlands viaduct was a major news
story in the region. This account draws from stories in the *Jer-*

sey Journal, the *Hudson Dispatch,* and the *Newark Evening News.*

8. The Nightstick Must Prevail

137   Accounts of the Skyway murder trail are available from the *Jersey Journal,* the *Hudson Dispatch,* and the *Newark Evening News.* A lengthy search for a transcript of the trial itself proved fruitless.

139   *Campbell told the court he had endured . . .* "Ironworker's 'Confession' In," *Newark Evening News,* December 7, 1932.

143   *"the nightstick must prevail"* Hague's declaration comes from "Hague Orders War on Labor Rackets," *New York Times,* May 2, 1934.

146   *Brandle and four executives . . .* "Brandle and His Business Group Must Pay $34,250," *Jersey Journal,* May 17, 1939.

148   *Incoming mail was routinely opened . . .* Dorsett, *Franklin D. Roosevelt and the City Bosses,* p. 103.

148   *This prompted Socialist leader Norman Thomas . . .* Norman Thomas filed a lawsuit against Hague over the incident, but dropped it after a few years as his legal costs mounted and the likelihood of penetrating Hague's judicial armor diminished. See Swanberg, *Norman Thomas,* pp. 223–224.

149   *When that didn't work, he reached out to his gangster buddy . . .* Hague's relationship with Zwillman and the dustup in Newark are dealt with by Warren Grover in *Nazis in Newark,* p. 224.

150   *From the top of the stairs, the screaming came . . .* Donald B. Robinson, "I Was in Journal Square," *New Republic,* May 25, 1938.

153   *Luke Grant, who had already analyzed . . .* Tin Rasenberger, *High Steel,* p. 121.

9. Death Avenue

155   The dedication of the Pulaski Skyway received extensive coverage in the *Jersey Journal,* the *Hudson Dispatch,* and the *Newark Evening News.* Details are drawn from all three.

158   The phrase "Hague's dachshund-faced style of public speak-

ing" belongs to Bob Leach of the Jersey City Free Public Library. He uses it in his writings for the Frank Hague Project.

162 The mayor's court testimony in defense of the Skyway truck ban is mentioned in "Mayor Hague on Stand," *New York Times*, April 14, 1934.

164 The excellent Web resource NYCRoads.com has a thorough write-up on the West Side Highway, http://www.nycroads .com/roads/west-side.

10. Steel and Ghosts

169 *There is great affection . . .* "At 60, the Pulaski Skyway Draws Admiration and Criticism," *New York Times*, October 10, 1993.

172 Details of the construction of the New Jersey Turnpike are taken from *The New Jersey Turnpike* by Michael Lapolla and Thomas A. Suszka, and from *Looking for America on the New Jersey Turnpike* by Angus Gillespie and Michael Aaron Rockland.

174 *Teddy Brandle remained in Jersey City . . .* "Brandle Tells of Big Money Days," *Jersey Journal*, March 25, 1941.

177 *The session was actually a gala retirement party . . .* Smith, *The Powerticians*, pp. 180–82.

179 *"The old convoy had started . . ."* Eisenhower, *At Ease*, pp. 166–67.

180 *Kenny always emphasized . . .* Karcher, *New Jersey's Multiple Municipal Madness*, p. 188.

182 *There's a wonderful anecdote . . .* Fleming tells this anecdote in Goldensohn and Cohen, *The Life and Times of Frank Hague*.

183 *"I never thought you two bastards . . ."* Smith, *The Powerticians*, p. 215.

BIBLIOGRAPHY

Books

The Eighth Wonder. New York: B. F. Sturtevant, 1927.

Adamic, Louis. *Dynamite: The Story of Class Violence in America.* New York: Viking Press, 1934.

Barker, Richard M., and Jay A. Puckett. *Design of Highway Bridges.* New York: John Wiley & Sons, 1997.

Bernstein, Irving. *The Lean Years: A History of the American Worker 1920–1933.* New York: Da Capo Press, 1960.

Condit, Carl W. *American Building Art: The Twentieth Century.* New York: Oxford University Press, 1961.

Connors, Richard J. *A Cycle of Power.* Metuchen, N.J.: Scarecrow Press, 1971.

Cunningham, John T. *Newark.* Newark, N.J.: New Jersey Historical Society, 1966.

———. *New Jersey: America's Main Road.* New York: Doubleday, 1976.

Davies, Pete. *American Road: The Story of an Epic Transcontinental Journey at the Dawn of the Motor Age.* New York: Henry Holt, 2002.

Dorsett, Lyle W. *Franklin D. Roosevelt and the City Bosses.* Port Washington, N.Y.: Kennikat Press, 1977.

Eisenhower, Dwight D. *At Ease: Stories I Tell to Friends.* New York: Doubleday Books, 1967.

Farley, James A. *Behind the Ballots: The Personal History of a Politician.* New York: Harcourt, Brace, 1938.

Fleming, Thomas. *Mysteries of My Father: An Irish-American Memoir.* New York: John Wiley & Sons, 2006.

———. *New Jersey: A Bicentennial History.* New York: W. W. Norton, 1977.

French, Kenneth. *Railroads of Hoboken and Jersey City.* Charleston, S.C.: Arcadia Publishing, 2002.

Gillespie, Angus K., and Michael Aaron Rockland. *Looking for America on the New Jersey Turnpike.* New Brunswick, N.J.: Rutgers University Press, 1993.

Goldensohn, Martin, and David Steven Cohen. *The Life and Times of Frank Hague.* Trenton: New Jersey Historical Commission and NJN Radio, 2001.

Grover, Warren. *Nazis in Newark.* New Brunswick, N.J.: Transaction Publishers, 2003.

Hokanson, Drake. *The Lincoln Highway: Main Street Across America.* Iowa City: University of Iowa Press, 1988.

Horan, James D. *The Desperate Years: A Pictorial History of the Thirties.* New York: Crown Publishers, 1962.

Johnson, Nelson. *Boardwalk Empire: The Birth, High Times, and Corruption of Atlantic City.* Meford, N.J.: Plexus Publishing, 2002.

Karcher, Alan J. *New Jersey's Multiple Municipal Madness.* New Brunswick, N.J.: Rutgers University Press, 1998.

Katcher, Leo. *The Big Bankroll: The Life and Times of Arnold Rothstein.* New York: Da Capo Press, 1994.

Lapolla, Michael, and Thomas A. Suszka. *The New Jersey Turnpike.* Charleston, S.C.: Arcadia Publishing, 2005.

Lavis, Fred. *Memoirs.* Unpublished manuscript, no date. Lavis family collection.

Mappen, Marc. *Jerseyana: The Underside of New Jersey History.* New Brunswick: Rutgers University Press, 1992.

McKean, Dayton David. *The Boss: The Hague Machine in Action.* Boston: Houghton Mifflin, 1940.

McWilliams, Leroy. *Parish Priest: A Man of God Tells His Story.* New York: McGraw-Hill, 1953.

Mysak, Joe, with Judith Schiffer. *Perpetual Motion: The Illustrated History of the Port Authority of New York and New Jersey.* Los Angeles: General Publishing Group, 1997.

Petroski, Henry. *Engineers of Dreams: Great Bridge Builders and the Spanning of America.* New York: Random House, 1996.

———. *Success Through Failure: The Paradox of Design.* Princeton, N.J.: Princeton University Press, 2006.

Rasenberger, Jim. *High Steel: The Daring Men Who Built the World's Greatest Skyline.* New York: HarperCollins, 2004.

Riordan, William L. *Plunkitt of Tammany Hall: A Series of Very Plain Talks on Very Practical Politics.* New York: Signet Classics, 1995 (originally published in 1905).

Seidman, Harold. *Labor Czars: A History of Labor Racketeering.* New York: Liveright Publishing, 1938.

Slayton, Robert A. *Empire Statesman: The Rise and Redemption of Al Smith.* New York: Free Press, 2001.

Smith, Thomas F. X. *The Powerticians.* Secaucus, N.J.: Lyle Stuart, 1982.

Sullivan, Robert. *The Meadowlands: Wilderness Adventures at the Edge of a City.* New York: Charles Scribner's Sons, 1998.

Swanberg, W. A. *Norman Thomas: The Last Idealist.* New York: Charles Scribner's Sons, 1976.

Troy, Leo. *Organized Labor in New Jersey.* Princeton, N.J.: D. Van Nostrand, 1965.

Wellington, Arthur Mellen. *The Economic Theory of the Location of Railways.* New York: John Wiley & Sons, 1908.

White, E. B. *Farewell to Model T/From Sea to Shining Sea.* New York: Little Bookroom, 2003.

Key Articles

Lavis, Fred. "Economic Theory of Highway Location." *Roads and Streets,* October 1927.

———. "Highways as Elements of Transportation." *Transactions of the American Society of Civil Engineers* 95 (1931).

McCahon, Mary, and Sandra G. Johnston. "Final Route One Extension National Register Nomination," February 9, 2005. On file with New Jersey Historic Preservation Office, Trenton, N.J.

McCarten, John. "Evolution of a Problem Child." *New Yorker,* February 12/19, 1938.

Mitchell, Joseph. "The Mohawks in High Steel." *Up in the Old Hotel.* New York: Vintage, 1993.

Reddan, Frank A. "A Super Viaduct." *Scientific American,* August 1932.

TAMS Consultants. "Routes U.S. 1 & 9 Corridor Historic Engineering Survey: Historical Narrative and Assessment of Significance and Integrity," August 1991. On file with New Jersey Historic Preservation Office, Trenton, N.J.

Wittles, David. "The Hague Machine." *New York Post,* February 7, 1938.

INDEX